PATH TO THE
STARS

PATH TO THE
STARS

*My Journey from Girl Scout
to Rocket Scientist*

SYLVIA ACEVEDO

CLARION BOOKS
Houghton Mifflin Harcourt
Boston New York

Clarion Books
3 Park Avenue
New York, New York 10016

Clarion Books is an imprint of Houghton Mifflin Harcourt Publishing Company.

hmhco.com

The text was set in Janson MT Std.

Library of Congress Cataloging-in-Publication Data
Names: Acevedo, Sylvia, author.
Title: Path to the stars : my journey from Girl Scout to rocket scientist / Sylvia Acevedo.
Description: Boston; New York : Clarion Books, Houghton Mifflin Harcourt, [2018] | Audience: Age 10–12. | Audience: Grade 4 to 6.
Identifiers: LCCN 2018005790 | ISBN 9781328809568 (hardcover)
Subjects: LCSH: Acevedo, Sylvia—Juvenile literature. |
Women engineers—United States—Biography—Juvenile literature. |
Engineers—United States—Biography—Juvenile literature. |
Hispanic American women—Biography—Juvenile literature. |
Hispanic American scientists—Biography—Juvenile literature. |
Girl Scouts of the United States of America—Officials and employees.
Classification: LCC TA157.5 .A24 2018 | DDC 369.463092 [B]—dc23
LC record available at https://lccn.loc.gov/2018005790

Printed in the United States of America
DOC 10 9 8 7 6 5 4 3 2 1
4500722659

To my mother,
Ofelia Monge Acevedo,
and my Tía,
Angélica Monge

INTRODUCTION

When I was young, my favorite toy was a kaleidoscope. I'd stand in our backyard and hold it up to the full moon, watching the colored shapes tumble into new patterns that were never the same twice. When I tired of one combination, I'd just twist the cylinder, and a new one, totally different, would settle into view. Then I'd lower the kaleidoscope and see the bright moon shining over the New Mexico desert, so large and low it seemed I could walk over and touch it.

Sometimes the patterns in my kaleidoscope reminded me of the colors and shapes in my world: Mami's favorite dress, Papá's stack of library books, the blanket in my sister

Laura's crib. At other times they were more abstract, not like anything in my day-to-day life, but beautiful all the same. When I was older, I would sometimes pick up my old toy and find that the colorful patterns called to mind the structure of molecules or a schematic plan for an electrical circuit. My understanding of the world had become more sophisticated as I had grown up; the kaleidoscope hadn't changed, but I had.

I've come a long way since those nights, standing outside in our yard under a blanket of brilliant stars. When I was in elementary school, most girls I knew wanted to grow up to raise a family and keep house. Few of them planned on going to college and finding a job they loved. If they pictured themselves earning a living, it was never as a mechanic or an engineer or a scientist, jobs they — and everyone else we knew — considered to be men's work.

When I was in second grade, something happened that changed my life: a classmate suggested I come with her to an after-school group for girls. I loved it from the very first moment. The group was called the Brownies, and I learned that they were part of a larger organization called the Girl Scouts.

The Girl Scouts taught me how to organize and plan for the future. Over the years, they helped me learn the connection between cooking and science, between selling cookies and managing my money. Most important, the Girl Scouts encouraged my dreams of college and taught me that I could create my own opportunities.

I liked math and science, so I decided to give engineering a try. I ended up working as a rocket scientist and for computer companies in the early days of the Internet. I started my own company and, eventually, even got to be on a presidential commission, attending many meetings at the White House, where I met President Obama, cabinet secretaries, senators, members of Congress, military generals and admirals, as well as members of the Supreme Court. I joined the national board of the Girl Scouts so I could help the organization that had given *me* so much help. Then I was invited to serve as their chief executive officer.

I talk to young people just like you all the time—and I listen to you too. I know that even today, kids and teens are still told what you *can't* do. Sometimes you're told you can't be good at math or other hard subjects, when all you really need is more help to understand them. Or you're told you

can't have a fulfilling career, when you just need help apply-
ing to college. The worst is when you think you can't realize
your dreams at all, no matter how hard you work. That's just
not true. Sometimes you need a little boost to understand
what you're capable of—and to help you take responsibility
for your aspirations. I hope my story helps you dream big
dreams and make those dreams come true.

CHAPTER 1

Born in the Shadow of Mount Rushmore

My Papá wasn't much for telling stories. He liked facts and information. If you asked him about the Mexican Revolution or about the freezing point of water, he'd go on all day, sounding grown-up and important, like the men who read the news on television. Mami was the storyteller in our family—as long as the subject was people. I thought she must know everybody in the world—who their family was, where they came from, and what they did all day.

Still, my father had one story that I always loved to hear. "Papá, tell me about the hospital!" I'd beg him.

Sometimes it took a few tries, but he'd finally look up from his book.

"The hospital," he'd repeat, his voice thoughtful. "I drove by it every day, but I'd never gone inside. It was not far from Ellsworth Air Force Base, where we lived when I was stationed in South Dakota, less than an hour from Mount Rushmore."

He would always start by telling me about his time in the army. Papá was proud of his army service, so part of the story was about how he'd entered the army after the Korean War as a lieutenant in the Air Defense Artillery.

"Your brother, Mario, was already two years old," Papá would continue, finally getting to the important part of the story. "Once we knew the new baby was about to be born, I brought Mami to the hospital. We all went inside, even Mario.

"The nurse told me Mami would need some time and I should come back later. So I went home to the base where we lived and left Mario with a neighbor. When I got back to the hospital, they said it would be a while before I could see your mother."

In those days, fathers stayed in a waiting room while

their babies were being born, and new babies were usually brought to the nursery, not kept with their mothers. It was a long time before a nurse came out to tell Papá that Mami was fine, but she was asleep. The nurse said Papá could see his baby.

When he got to the nursery, Papá looked through a big window and saw rows of metal cribs with clear plastic sides, each crib just big enough for one tiny infant. Some of the babies had blond hair, and some had brown hair or no hair at all. Nearly all of them had fair skin. Only one baby had very dark hair.

"That was me!" I'd say. "I wasn't even one day old." I knew Papá had had no trouble picking me out in the nursery because I looked like him, even though he was a grown man in an army uniform and I was a little baby wrapped in a white blanket. He knew right away I was his. And I was sure that I knew right away that he was my Papá.

Papá would nod at that point in the story, and sometimes he'd even smile. I'd wait for him to say something else, but usually his nose would go right back into his book.

I was always excited to hear this story, but over the years, I came to understand more about what living in

South Dakota had been like for Mami. Papá's family was from Mexico, but he had grown up in Texas. He had gotten all of his schooling, including college, in the United States, and he spoke English well. After graduation, he was fulfilling his army ROTC commitment as an officer stationed in South Dakota, and he went off to work every day at the missile battalion protecting Ellsworth Air Force Base.

But Mami had grown up in Parral, Mexico, in the state of Chihuahua, and didn't understand a word of English. The neighbors gave her baby clothes and thick winter coats for the brutal South Dakota winters, but they didn't speak Spanish. Papá was often away overnight, and she was alone with two small children.

I remember Mami singing a song about Marranito, a little pig, while counting our fingers and toes. Mario and I loved having her undivided attention, and she loved playing with us and making us laugh. But Mami had no adults to talk with except Papá.

Even the landscape was not what Mami was used to: tree-covered hills and rolling plains instead of a desert sprinkled with cacti and spiky plants. The summers were very hot, with black flies everywhere, and the winters were freezing cold. Only the stars were the same as she remembered from home.

Mami never liked to complain, but she must have been lonely. She was overjoyed when Papá's tour of duty was up after two years and he was discharged from the army. Now we were free to move to a new home.

Mami and Papá packed up their beige 1955 Ford and drove one thousand miles south to Las Cruces, New Mexico, where we moved in with Tía Alma, Papá's older sister, and her family, the Barbas: Uncle Sam Barba and my cousins Debbie, Cathy, and Sammy. I don't know why we used the Spanish "tía" for Tía Alma but the Anglo "uncle" for Uncle Sam. That's just the way it was. My father's mother, Abuelita Juanita, lived with the Barbas too. When we moved in, Mario was four years old and I was just two.

From the first day, I remember the babble of voices, the adults speaking Spanish, a swirl of words and song and argument and stories and laughter, with my mother somehow always at the center. My cousins spoke a mix of English and Spanish, but Mario and I spoke only Spanish at that time.

I remember eating breakfast in the family room, sitting

at the table with Mario and my cousins, each of us with our small glass of juice and bowl of cereal. Mario and I slept in this room too, because all of the bedrooms were full.

The house was crowded, but I didn't mind, because there was always someone to play with. Every day after breakfast, we'd tumble outside and chase one another through the yard and the back alley, discovering the world. I remember running to catch up with Mario and my older cousins, running for the sheer joy of speed and the wind on my face.

For my father, who grew up with one much older sister, the noise of five small children was a trial. He loved us, but he would often spend his afternoons at the library instead of playing with us or helping my mother around the house.

Once he found work, rather than wearing his army uniform, Papá dressed like the other men in our new neighborhood, donning dress slacks and a button-down shirt and tie for his job at New Mexico State University, where he was a chemist in the physical science laboratories. My aunt, uncle, and grandmother went to work too. My aunt was a schoolteacher, and my uncle worked at White Sands Missile

Range. My grandmother had a job at a clothing store. My mother was left to keep house and look after all the children. It was a lot of responsibility for her.

Mami had grown up poor, with thirteen brothers and sisters. Her school days ended after the sixth grade, but she'd wanted more education. She took a typing class and made her way north to the border city of Juárez, Mexico, when she was sixteen, hoping to work as a secretary. She didn't find a job in Juárez, but she would regularly cross the pedestrian bridge to El Paso, in Texas, where she worked cleaning homes.

Mami made many friends in El Paso. She was only nineteen when she met Papá. By the time they moved to Las Cruces, they had been married for almost five years. Mami was twenty-four and Papá was twenty-six.

My aunt and uncle's house was small, but it had soft carpets, and a baby grand piano shoehorned into the living room. With her hardscrabble background, my mother thought my aunt, uncle, and grandmother put on aristocratic airs. She felt they looked down on her for having grown up in poverty. Papá was a college graduate, and his sister, Tía Alma, was too. Mami knew his family would have preferred that he'd married someone with more education than she had.

Papá would have been content to stay at his sister's house, as crowded as it was, but Mami wanted her own home. In the afternoons, when my grandmother returned from her job, my mother would take me for walks and look for signs that said CASA PARA RENTAR, meaning a house was for rent.

It wasn't long before my mother found a new house for us, and we moved out of my aunt and uncle's home. Now we lived less than a mile away, on Solano Street, a busy thoroughfare next to an arroyo, a steep, dry gully that flooded after the heavy summer rains.

Our new house was made of cinder blocks and painted green on the outside. It was tiny, with barely enough room for the four of us and Manchas, our dog. There were two small bedrooms, a bathroom, a kitchen with just enough space for a table, and a living room with a foldout couch that took up the entire room when it was open. The bedroom Mario and I shared had a closet, two small beds, and a round hooked rug where we played with our toys. We liked to go outside and play in the arroyo, where there was room to run around.

Our new next-door neighbor raised chickens, and she sold Mami fresh eggs. Every Sunday my father would buy a chicken from her, and she'd slaughter it so Mami could cook it for dinner after church. Friends from church gave us some furniture, and Mami shopped around for more, using layaway plans at stores since we didn't have a credit card.

My mother was very thrifty. She budgeted carefully to be able to buy a green Formica kitchen table and chairs, as well as our other new furniture.

Soon after we moved in, the living room became even more crowded, because my mother's younger sister, Tía Angélica, arrived from Mexico to stay with us. She had come to help out because Mami was going to have a baby.

Tía Angélica was young and pretty, with hair she swept up into a ponytail that swung around when she turned her head. She adored my mother, and Mami was overjoyed to have her little sister living with us. They talked and laughed and sang all day long.

Tía Angélica didn't want to be a burden on our family. She helped Mami and quickly found work cleaning Tía

Alma's house, as well as other people's homes. She loved Mario and me, and she praised us, making us feel special and very smart. She'd take us to the toy store and buy us something with her earnings or treat us to a showing at the Mexican movie theater, where an actor named Cantinflas would make us laugh and laugh.

At night, Tía Angélica slept on the couch. There was a crib squeezed between the sofa and the coffee table, and Tía Angélica and Mami unpacked Mario's and my old baby clothes while I watched, fascinated.

I was four years old now, and while I didn't much care for dolls—I had one, named Óscar, a Christmas present from my grandmother—I wanted to see the little brother or sister whose clothes were no bigger than Óscar's. Even though I had seen pictures of me as a baby, I had trouble imagining another baby living in our house. Would it cry all day? What would it be like to have a new brother or a sister? What would its name be? Most important, would the new baby be a boy, like Mario, or a girl, like me? I thought Papá would probably prefer another boy, but I didn't want to ask him. Mami, smiling, refused to say which kind of baby she'd like best. We would just have to wait and see.

One morning, my mother wasn't in the kitchen. Instead, Tía Angélica was singing to the radio while she poured my orange juice. Smiling at Mario and me, she told us we had a new baby sister named Laura. Mami and Laura would be in the hospital for a few days, and Tía Angélica would take care of us.

Every day while Mami was gone, Tía Angélica would take Mario and me downtown to Woolworths so we could buy a toy, or she would play games with us, or sometimes she would just sit in the sun, painting her fingernails pink, while we ran in the arroyo.

I soon came to love Tía Angélica, but even so, it seemed like a long time before Mami and Papá brought Laura home. On the day my baby sister came home from the hospital, Mario and I crowded into the living room to see her. Manchas was also very curious. As we took turns holding Laura, he sniffed her all over. I took a couple of sniffs too. She smelled a little like sour milk, I decided. She had dark hair, just like I did, but hers was curly, and she gazed at us with dark, curious eyes.

We all loved Laura, but Manchas became my sister's protector. At night, he would circle her crib several times before dropping down in front of it and closing his eyes. That way, he could guard the crib even while he was asleep.

Not long after Laura was born, my father came home early one day and said he'd been fired. He'd been having trouble at his job, and now New Mexico State University didn't want him to work for them anymore. At the time, I didn't know what this meant, but when I was older, I came to understand that my father was fired because he hadn't taken his job seriously enough. He would get to work late, or leave early, or not listen when his bosses told him what to do, so he'd make mistakes. He didn't pay attention to details. In fact, he had been sloppy, which was dangerous since he worked with chemicals.

In our tiny home with three young children, it was a tense time, though I didn't know why. I thought Papá might stay home now and play with us. Instead, he spent his days at the library and much of the weekends at his sister's house.

Soon Tía Alma's husband, Uncle Sam, helped my father get an interview at White Sands Missile Range. To everyone's relief, Papá was offered a new job there as an analytical chemist. Now he got up early to take the bus to work. He left before Mario and I were awake.

At age twenty-eight, being fired had made my father realize that he had to take responsibility for his family. He had a wife and three children who depended on him. He vowed that he would take this new job seriously. He got to the laboratory on time and worked hard. He took pride in his new position.

Papá's job at the missile range paid better than his old job, so my mother started looking for another house for us to rent, one not located on a busy street, with enough space for our family to grow.

Mami had always warned us about cars, which was why we played in the arroyo and not in the street, but unfortunately, Manchas must not have been listening. Shortly after Laura was born, Manchas wandered onto the busy street and was hit by a car. Mario and I cried and cried, but there was nothing anyone could do, and Papá and Uncle Sam buried him in the desert.

Soon after that, Mami told us she'd found a house in another part of town, on Griggs Street, which wasn't even paved. It was close enough that we could still walk to our church and see our friends in the old neighborhood. Our new home had three bedrooms and a large backyard, with several trees big enough to climb.

Mami felt at home on Griggs Street. From the moment we'd moved to New Mexico from South Dakota two years ago, she'd been happy to be back in a place where people spoke Spanish. Like us, most of our neighbors had friends and relatives who lived in Mexico. Now, in our third home in Las Cruces, she had a house roomy enough for our growing family. She thought we could stay there for a long time.

In our new home, Mario had his own bedroom, and I shared a room with Laura. The weather was nearly always sunny, and people spilled out of their houses into the yards and the park down the street. My mother always had food ready for visitors, and she quickly made many friends.

Mario and I made friends too. There were children everywhere. If you wanted to find someone to play with, you just had to go outside.

After we moved to Griggs Street, my father bought a

car to replace our old Ford, a used Rambler. We loved our new car, which was roomy and had a back seat that folded down. My father liked being able to drive to the missile range's checkpoint. There he would park and catch a bus to his job, another twenty-six miles away on the other side of the Organ Mountains. Driving over the mountain pass would have put a strain on the engine, and my father didn't want to wear it out. Besides, he liked reading the *El Paso Times* on the morning bus ride, though he read other newspapers in the library. He didn't think much of the local *Las Cruces Sun-News*.

My mother had a beautiful voice, and she sang when she was happy. After we moved to Griggs Street, I would wake up in the morning to hear her singing along to the radio. There were no Spanish language stations in Las Cruces at this time, so she listened to the Spanish radio stations from nearby Juárez, Mexico. I loved it when her favorite songs, such as "Qué rico el mambo" or "Cielito lindo," came on. She would twirl Mario or me to the peppy music until we were dizzy, then scoop up baby Laura in her arms and dance around the kitchen, singing with joy about the rich mambo dance or someone she loved.

Mami had an impish sense of humor, and she loved to play pranks. I remember she would go out on the roof to call for Mario or me when we were playing in the yard. We'd hear her voice, and before we realized where she was, she'd jump right down beside us, startling us. She'd laugh, so we'd know we weren't in any trouble, and before we knew it, we'd be laughing too.

Las Cruces was a very small town when we moved there. Most of the streets were unpaved. Vendors sold fruit and vegetables off horse- or mule-drawn carts, and stray dogs roamed free. When you wanted to make a telephone call, you would pick up the receiver and dial only four numbers to reach anyone. And when you had to mail a letter, you just wrote the family's name and street address on the envelope. You didn't need to bother with the city name or Zip Code if they lived in Las Cruces.

To me, the days were like magic. My mother tried to make plans, but she was always hospitable when visitors appeared without warning and changed the shape of our day. On the weekends, friends and family would come over, and we would enjoy long afternoons that stretched into evenings of fun and food. Left to himself, my father would have passed the weekends reading, but he knew it was important to put down his book and spend time with our family and visitors.

Papá was stricter than Mami was. When we misbehaved, Papá would sometimes spank us. I would cry loudly, even when I knew I'd been wrong or naughty. Papá was mean, I thought, even though I knew I loved him. But all the kids in our neighborhood got spanked sometimes.

Mami didn't spank us, though. Instead, if two of us were fighting, she'd lock us in the bathroom together, telling us not to come out until we were friends again. Mami knew we'd resolve our differences just to get out of that tiny room.

Before long, I thought my mother must know every family in our neighborhood. She knew who needed help, whether it was a meal or baby-sitting or a trip to the store. She knew who was having a baby and needed a crib, and whose baby was sleeping in a bed now, so the family had a crib they could spare. Mami loved to cook for visitors. And I loved our close-knit community, where every day seemed to bring us friends and get-togethers.

I especially loved birthday parties, where we all took turns swinging a heavy stick at the piñata hanging from a tree in the park or in someone's yard. When one of the children finally succeeded in breaking open the piñata, we'd all swarm around to gather the candy that rained onto the ground. After the piñata, we'd have colorful birthday cake and ice cream, and my mother would serve her special punch: Kool-Aid mixed with 7-Up soda and slices of orange. Before everyone left, Mami would lead the guests in "Las mañanitas," the Mexican birthday song, singing the verses as everyone else joined in on the chorus. Except for Christmas, I didn't think anything could be better than a birthday party.

Now that he had a reliable car, my father would drive to El Paso, forty-five miles away, to visit his father, Abuelito Mario. My father's parents had divorced when he was eight years old, and my grandfather had started another family. My father dutifully visited him every two weeks. He'd take his mother, Abuelita Juanita, with him and drop her at her sister's house before visiting my grandfather.

El Paso was considered a big city compared to Las Cruces. A trip there was a treat for our whole family. We would cross the Mexican border into Juárez to shop for items that were priced lower in Mexico or not available in the United States. We would look in the big department stores in El Paso, like the Popular, which my mother loved for its fashionable clothing. Then we would sometimes visit Abuelito Mario before picking up my grandmother at her sister's home. I loved our trips to the big city, but usually Papá went to El Paso with only his mother. When I was little, this didn't bother me. Papá was gone most of the time, and I didn't really understand the difference between his being at work and visiting his father. But when I was a little older, I too wanted to see my grandfather.

I remember one particular Saturday when Papá told us we would all be coming with him to El Paso. Mami made sure we were wearing our best clothes, and I thought she looked beautiful in a flowered dress she usually saved for church. We piled into the car for the hour-long drive.

On this visit, my grandmother didn't come. We went shopping and then stopped by Abuelito Mario's house to visit. But my grandfather and his family weren't there, so we sat down on the front steps to wait.

After a little while, my mother suggested that we leave, since it was getting late. My father said no. He said he always visited his father every other Saturday afternoon, so Abuelito Mario was expecting him and would surely arrive any minute.

My mother could see that this visit was important to my father, and we ended up waiting several hours for my grandfather to show up. When Mario and I grew restless and began to complain, my mother let us explore the neighborhood, telling us not to go too far. We went around the block several times, investigating the houses, a church, and a small corner store. Finally, tired, we joined my parents and Laura on the front steps of my grandfather's house, and as the shadows began to lengthen, Abuelito Mario, his wife, and their daughters finally arrived.

By now, Mario and I were famished.

If they had been visiting us, my mother would have served them an entire meal without even asking if they were hungry. But my abuelito and his wife didn't seem all that interested in seeing us. We sat around awkwardly while Papá and his father talked. Even though we hadn't eaten since breakfast, we children had to content ourselves with some cookies and a shared soda, and that was only after Mami asked.

I was surprised that my grandfather's family seemed to think we were a bother. When we visited with my cousins in Las Cruces or in Mexico, all of us would run around outside and play. But my grandfather's daughters, who were my father's stepsisters, were older than we were and didn't want to play with us.

On the drive home, my father kept talking about the visit with his wonderful father, and my mother didn't say much at all, which was unlike her. It was as if Papá were describing an entirely different visit than the one we had just experienced.

My mother was quiet on the car ride home, which was unlike her. Normally after a get-together, she would have discussed the people we had just spent time with and the things we had done that day. This time, she was being very kind and gentle with my father, not disagreeing with him, even though it was clear to me that my grandfather had not been excited to see us. I remember her saying "Sí, sí, sí," agreeing when my father talked about how smart and wonderful my grandfather was.

I thought my father wanted attention from my grandfather, that he was acting the way Mario and I did when we would say "Papá, Papá, Papá," getting louder until he looked up from his book. That was not how Papá normally acted, and he certainly was not like that with his mother, my abuelita Juanita.

We didn't return as a family to visit my grandfather for many years. Although my father continued to speak reverently about his father, we didn't stop at Abuelito Mario's house when we went to El Paso to go shopping. As a result, I didn't really get to know my father's stepsisters. I was very curious about them, but my father rarely answered my questions.

Papá still visited his father regularly, but we never asked to go with him. He always went without us, just as he'd done in the past. After that unwelcoming visit, Mami, Mario, Laura, and I stayed home.

Mami, Papá, and me, 1960

Mario and me, around 1960

CHAPTER 2

Preschool for Mario and Me

The Spanish Baptist church, La Primera Iglesia Bautista, was not only our spiritual home, but also the center of our family's social life.

Many of our neighbors, and most other families we knew who were from Mexico were Catholic. We were Baptist. My father's family had converted to Protestantism in Mexico in the 1800s. When they fled Mexico during the revolution, they found a church home in the Spanish Baptist church in El Paso, Texas. My great-grandfather became a pastor there.

My mother's mother, Abuelita Leonor, had been widowed young. My mother's father had been a Jehovah's

Witness, and in time, my grandmother explored other religions. When Mami moved to Juárez, she in turn investigated different churches that offered services in Spanish. She first met my father and his family at the Spanish Baptist church in El Paso on Valentine's Day.

When we moved to Las Cruces, the Spanish Baptist church had a full service that was all in Spanish, and my mother felt comfortable there. Most of my parents' friends attended services at the church as well. One of my favorite photographs shows my mother, both my grandmothers, and two of my aunts at a meeting of the Women's Auxiliary, a group of women who did volunteer work for the church. The photo was taken when my mother's mother, who lived in Chihuahua, Mexico, visited us after Laura was born.

The sanctuary in our church was small. The center was filled with pews, and there were three side rooms that served as overflow areas or makeshift classrooms. In the front, behind the choir's pews and preacher's pulpit, was the baptismal font. Behind the font was the vestry, a room where the choir robes were kept. That space was off-limits to children, so of course we were fascinated with it, and we made up crazy stories about what might be inside. If we got bored at the church when my mother was busy with auxiliary work or chatting with her friends during Bible study, we'd play in the nearby park.

Even though our family and all of our neighbors in Las Cruces spoke Spanish, Mami had not forgotten what it had been like in South Dakota, when she couldn't understand the language everyone else was speaking. My father spoke both English and Spanish well, and that was what my mother wanted for Mario and me.

Mami had made friends with Hermana Amelia Díaz, a missionary who lived in a cottage on the church grounds. Hermana Díaz spoke English and Spanish and sang in a high, warbly, birdlike voice. She always wore her hair pulled back, and she seemed very strict. She spoke in polite, formal language, and unlike most adults I knew, she didn't smile when she talked to children. I was a little scared of her.

One spring day, not long after Laura was born, Mami invited Hermana Díaz over to our house. Mami set the table with her prettiest napkins and served her guest cake with lemon-yellow icing and coffee. Mami never drank tea. Tea made her think of her childhood in Mexico, when they were so poor that they couldn't afford coffee. Instead, they had drunk tea, water flavored with dried herbs that my Abuelita Leonor had collected by the roadside. My mother always said that tea reminded her of being poor. Every morning, Mami relished her cup of coffee.

Now Mami welcomed Hermana Díaz into our home with pride. The two women sat drinking their coffee, chatting about church and the neighborhood. Then Mami told Hermana Díaz that she had learned that the teachers at the local school, Bradley Elementary, would speak to us in English, not Spanish. Would Hermana Díaz be willing to teach English to Mario and me so we'd be ready when we started school?

I knew that Mario would be starting first grade in August, a few months away. But I was two years younger and wouldn't be in school for a long time as there was no kindergarden at Bradley in those days. I would have plenty of time to learn English with Hermana Díaz.

Hermana Díaz looked thoughtful. She turned to my brother and me. "Are you willing to study and work hard?" she asked in Spanish.

Mario and I just nodded. I felt too shy to speak.

"Yes," Hermana Díaz told Mami. She would teach us.

We started preschool a few days later, in the morning after breakfast. The first day, Mami and Laura came with us, but after that, twice a week, Mario and I often would walk the three blocks to the church alone while Mami stayed home with Laura to start the day's housework.

At the time, Mario was six years old and I was four. No one ever questioned whether it was safe for my brother and me, young as we were, to walk around without an adult. Back then, it wasn't unusual for children as young as four to cross busy streets or to spend most of the day outside unsupervised. Even before they were old enough for elementary school, children were often sent to run errands several blocks away, buying groceries or even cigarettes for their parents.

From the first day, I knew that school was serious. Hermana Díaz had set up a classroom in an alcove of the church. She had found a little desk with a bench just big enough for my brother and me to sit on side-by-side. On the desk were two Big Chief writing tablets—notebooks with a picture of a Native American wearing a feather headdress on the red cover—and fat pencils that were easy to grip. There was an American flag in the corner of the room and, in the center, a blackboard easel with new sticks of white chalk and an eraser. Hermana Díaz had a chair so she could sit down while she worked with us.

Hermana Díaz was born in San Antonio, Texas, and she wanted us to be as proud of our American citizenship as she was of hers. On the first day, she told Mario and me that we would begin by saying the Pledge of Allegiance. I didn't know what that was.

Speaking in Spanish, Hermana Díaz told us to face the flag with our hands over our hearts. Confused, I put both hands on my chest.

Hermana Díaz reached over and adjusted my right hand so that it squarely covered my heart. She gently pushed my left hand down to my side. "Repeat after me," she said in English. Then she said the words in Spanish.

"I pledge allegiance to the flag..." she started, not stopping until Mario and I could both say the unfamiliar words in both languages.

Even after Hermana Díaz taught us the Pledge of Allegiance, I didn't know what it was for or why it was so important. I had never heard my parents recite the pledge, so

I figured it must have had something to do with learning English, even though I didn't really understand the difference between the two languages. We knew Papá spoke English at work, but Spanish was still the only language used in our home.

On the very first day of preschool, after we recited the Pledge of Allegiance, Hermana Díaz announced that we would learn our ABCs. I knew she meant the letters that I saw in Papá's books. Did she mean that once we knew what those letters were, we would be able to read?

I soon learned what she meant. That day and every day at school, after we recited the Pledge of Allegiance, we would sit at our desks and work on our ABCs. Hermana Díaz would say each new letter, and then she'd have us say it too, until she was satisfied with our English pronunciation.

Because Mario was older than I was, he had already learned some English from his friends in the neighborhood, so Hermana Díaz spent more time working with me. Even at that young age, I wanted to keep up with my brother. I would say the letters aloud and she would help me hold my oversize pencil and trace them on my Big Chief tablet.

I couldn't help wondering if the Big Chief could read what we were writing. If he were here, would he let me try on his feather headdress? My mother had told me stories about the Native American reservations in South Dakota. She even teased me sometimes, saying that she'd adopted me from one of them. Maybe the Big Chief was from South Dakota, I thought, though I didn't really know where that was.

Like Mami, Hermana Díaz loved to sing. To build our vocabulary in English, she taught us the song "Jesus Loves Me." I knew this song in Spanish as "Cristo me ama," so I was surprised and pleased to hear it in English with the exact same melody. English and Spanish words could represent the same things, I realized, as verse by verse, we learned the song in a new language. They could convey the same happy and sad emotions, too.

Mario had only a few lessons with Hermana Díaz before he started first grade at Bradley Elementary School, but I continued to see her twice a week. Mario and I had gone together to preschool, but now my mother usually walked with me, carrying Laura, and dropped me off at my classroom. Sometimes she'd leave and go home to start dinner, but often she'd stay and visit with a friend who lived near the church. When the class was over, Mami — or Tía Angélica on one of her frequent visits — would pick me up, or I'd go home on my own. Then it was my job to watch Laura while Mami did her chores or cooked our meals.

Hermana Díaz always started her lessons with the Pledge of Allegiance, and then she would drill me on what I had learned last time. I would recite the alphabet in English and write the letters on my tablet. Hermana Díaz would tell me something in Spanish and then repeat what she'd just said in English. She would make me repeat it too. She taught me to read in English but not in Spanish, and I never did learn to read more than basic Spanish.

After my reading lesson, Hermana Díaz would have me count as high as I could. I could already count a little bit in Spanish, telling myself "uno, dos, tres" as we walked the three blocks to church. Before long I could count in English, too. Soon I could count past one hundred, and I was counting everything I saw — people, trees, cars — in English *and* Spanish, chanting happily to myself in both languages. I found it exciting to practice two things, my new language and my counting skills, at the same time, and from those days, I developed a lifelong passion for counting and playing with numbers in my head.

While I was learning the alphabet, Mario was learning to read books in school. And because he could read books, he got to visit the library with my father. They would go off together on a Saturday, and my father would check out books for Mario on his library card. I wished I could go with them, but I knew I wouldn't be allowed. Mario was older and he was a boy, so he had privileges that I didn't have. And one of those privileges was to spend extra time with Papá. That was just the way things were.

I knew that the books my father borrowed from the library were in English. Mario was speaking English in school, too. We talked in Spanish when we played with our friends, but I noticed that the older children spoke English to one another. Increasingly, we spoke English with our cousins in Las Cruces, although we still spoke to my Abuel-ita Juanita in Spanish. And we spoke Spanish to my mother and Tía Angélica, too.

When Mario started first grade, my father began to speak to him in English, saying this would help him do bet-ter in school. I decided to speak to my father in English too. So while my father didn't take me to the library as he did Mario, he began to speak to me in English sometimes, and he corrected me when I got a word wrong. He and my mother spoke to each other only in Spanish. My mother under-stood very little English in those years, but she encouraged my father to talk to Mario and me in English.

Papá was gone most of the day, though, and he wasn't the kind of father who liked to play with young children. He was too impatient to spend much time talking with us. Still, he could sometimes be an ally. One time, Mario and I were jumping on the living room furniture and Tía Angé-lica started to scold us. Papá interrupted her, saying it wasn't her place to reprimand us. If we wanted to jump on the fur-niture, that was fine with him.

It wasn't until we were older that we had any real

conversations with Papá—in English or in Spanish. At that time, the only person who was teaching me how to read and write in English was Hermana Díaz. She was a good teacher and I respected her. As I got to know her better, I came to learn that while she was very strict and clear about her rules and expectations, she was affectionate and really did love children. Even so, she was quick to correct me and Mario, and immediately put an end to any horseplay in her class. Of course, once Mario started first grade, I was her only student. No other children from church families ever took lessons from her, even though my mother asked her friends if they'd like to have their children join me.

One day I saw something new on the wall of our classroom: a large, colorful poster covered with irregular shapes and lines that seemed to go in all directions. "This is a children's map of the United States," said Hermana Díaz. I didn't know what that was. I studied the map carefully while my teacher pointed out the states, rivers, oceans, and highways.

There were pictures on the map too. "This is where we are now, in the state of New Mexico," Hermana Díaz went on, pointing to a drawing of Native Americans standing outside an adobe building. I had heard my parents use the words "New Mexico," but I had never understood what they meant. "And this is where you were born," she said. "In South Dakota, nearly one thousand miles away." My teacher traced the lines on the map that outlined the different states. I wondered if we could see the lines marked on the ground outside.

I didn't remember anything of our time in South Dakota, but at home, we had a sugar bowl with a picture of Mount Rushmore on the side. I was fascinated by the four presidents whose faces were carved into the side of a mountain: George Washington, Thomas Jefferson, Theodore Roosevelt, and Abraham Lincoln. Even if I didn't completely understand who they were, I knew I had seen the enormous sculpture when I was a baby. From listening to Papá talking politics with Tía Alma and Uncle Sam, I even knew that John F. Kennedy was the president now. My mother loved to discuss the fashions worn by the First Lady, Jacqueline Kennedy. Was President Kennedy's face carved into a mountainside too?

Now, on the map, I saw a picture of the same four presidents whose faces were on Mount Rushmore in South

Dakota. I still didn't really know what a state was or the difference between New Mexico and Mexico. But everyone I knew had been born in Texas, New Mexico, or Mexico. I was the only person who'd been born somewhere far away, in another part of the United States!

I felt proud that I was learning English. I was also proud that I had seen Mount Rushmore, even if I didn't remember it. Maybe when I was grown up, I thought, I would drive my car there, and when I did, I would know how to speak English to anyone I met along the way—even the president.

Mario, Hermana Díaz, and me, around 1961

Me and Mario at Uncle Sam's house on Alamo Street, Las Cruces, around 1961

CHAPTER 3

The World Becomes a Dark and Scary Place

Laura-ca-louda, Laura-ca-louda," I chanted. My one-and-a-half-year-old sister looked up at me, her face happy and expectant. "Look at the pretty butterfly," I said, pointing at the bright orange creature fluttering over the flower garden.

"Butterfly," Laura repeated after me, pointing. "Laura," she added as she pointed at herself. My little sister loved her name.

From the moment she was born, Laura had a special hold on everyone's heart. She was in a hurry to keep up — with Mario and me, with our cousins, with anyone. She had never bothered to crawl, instead pulling herself up using tables and chairs so she could run after us. "Me run," she would say, holding her hands in the air as she sprinted away, giggling. She was very active, a happy child who lit up the room with her joy and energy.

Laura was in a hurry to talk, too. "Adiós," she'd say, looking at Mami. Then she'd turn to me and say, "Bye-bye!" She'd run away and come back to us a moment later, saying "Hola" and "Hello." One of her first words was "dress," and even as a toddler she showed a preference for girlie clothes. She would crawl onto my father's lap and babble, pretending to read aloud from his book.

She had my mother's vivaciousness and interest in people and my father's delight in learning. Everyone said Laura was the smartest of all of us. Her entire personality said, "I like people! Look at me!"

Laura and I were never far from Mami. All day, Mami would sing along to the radio, so we always knew where she was. Sometimes she'd pause in her work to twirl us around the kitchen. Mami and I would laugh and laugh as Laura danced until she was dizzy.

Except when I went to see Hermana Díaz, most days

after breakfast I would bolt outside to play in the back-yard, and Laura would toddle after me. My mother would remind me to be careful, watch out for Laura, and not get our clothes dirty. We were allowed to be outside without Mami as long as we stayed in the yard, where she could look through the window and see us.

Then one day when she was nineteen months old, Laura didn't wake up at her usual time. "Let her sleep," Mami told me. "She's just tired." Papá had gone to work early, as usual, and after Mario left for school, I decided to see if Laura was awake yet.

"Laura, Laura," I said, seeing that my sister's eyes were open. But Laura was hot and fretful, and she didn't seem to know I was there. "Laura, look, here's your baby," I said, holding her favorite doll, Cucá, in front of her. Abuelita Leonor had made Cucá for Laura, and normally my sister's eyes lit up when she saw her doll, but today she didn't re-spond. She just lay curled up on the bed, her eyes half open, burning with fever.

"Mami, something's wrong with Laura," I called, but Mami had already come into the bedroom with Tía

Angélica. Instead of answering me, Mami and my aunt looked at each other with worried eyes as they bent over my sister.

I knew something was really wrong when my mother snatched up Laura and ran outside. We didn't have a phone at home. Papá had the car at work, and anyway, Mami didn't know how to drive. She raced to our neighbor's house, rang the bell, and banged on their door. I ran after her, terrified at the sight of my mother crying and pleading for a ride to the emergency room. "¡Ayúdame, por favor. Mi hija está muy enferma. ¡Por favor, ayúdame!" *Help me, please. My daughter is very sick. Please, help me!*

Another neighbor heard my mother's anguished cries, and a few minutes later, her husband pulled up in their sedan. He leaned over to open the door, and my mother climbed in, clutching Laura's limp body to her chest, tears streaming down her face. Together, Tía Angélica and I watched them drive off. Even though my aunt was with me, I felt alone and scared. I didn't know what to do.

In another minute, we were surrounded by neighbors. Everyone wanted to know what had happened. My aunt just replied that Laura had a very high fever and was very sick. "Come, Sylvia," Tía Angélica said. "Let's go inside." I helped her with the breakfast dishes, the two of us wrapped in a cloud of worry.

Tía Angélica and I stayed in the house all morning and afternoon, not wanting to miss Mami if she came back, but she didn't come. It was a long, quiet day. Normally I would have spent the whole time outside, but instead I played quietly in my bedroom. When my mother and Laura returned, I wanted to be there so I could help take care of my sister.

When Mario came home from school and learned what had happened, his face crumpled, as if he was going to cry, and he went into his bedroom. Usually he'd change his clothes and go out to play, but that day, he just stayed in his room. Tía Angélica went in to talk with him, and afterward he came out into the living room and sat down next to me on the sofa.

In soft voices, we spoke about Laura. "Do you know what happened to her?" Mario asked me.

"No," I said. "Mami was crying and saying Laura needed a doctor right away. Laura's face was hot." But I sometimes had a fever when I was sick, and Mami didn't cry or take me to the hospital. Instead, she would rub Vicks VapoRub on my chest before I went to sleep, and I would wake up feeling better.

Mario picked up a book and started reading, so I went into the kitchen to watch Tía Angélica prepare our dinner.

Papá came home in time for dinner, but he was alone. He told us Mami had called him at work from the hospital, so he had driven straight there to see her and Laura. But when visiting hours were over, my mother had refused to leave Laura's side.

"Papá, how is Laura? When is Mami coming home?" I asked him, but he just shook his head and didn't answer me. The dinner table was quiet without Mami and Laura.

While Tía Angélica and I did the dishes, Tía Alma and Abuelita Juanita came over, and the adults spoke in hushed tones. "It's serious; it's meningitis," I heard Papá tell my aunt, though I didn't understand what that word meant. "Several people in the neighborhood have caught it, and a few have died. We don't know about Laura—" He saw me there and didn't finish the sentence.

After Tía Alma and my grandmother left, Papá told Tía Angélica to soak our clothes in boiling water to prevent further spread of the disease that had attacked Laura. It was evening, but my aunt started the old-time washer—a big tub and a hand crank—and washed all of our clothes, pajamas, towels, and sheets, even those that were already clean. She hung everything outside to dry, and late that night, yawning, I helped her make the beds with sheets that were crisp from the clothesline.

Our bedroom seemed eerily quiet with Laura in the hospital. Tía Angélica was preoccupied with folding and putting away the clothes, towels, and bed linens and didn't say much to me. I still didn't understand what had happened to Laura, or why she had gotten so sick.

The next day, I woke up to the sight of Laura's empty bed, and I remembered that my sister was in the hospital and my mother was with her.

Tía Angélica made our breakfast, and afterward, Mario and my father went off to school and work. Before he left, Papá told us he would go to the hospital after work, but he didn't say anything about when Mami and Laura would come home. Once again, I stayed inside all day with Tía Angélica. She forgot to turn on the radio, so our normally lively house was quiet. We were quiet too.

After lunch, later than the usual time, my aunt took me to my lesson with Hermana Díaz. Tía Angélica knew Hermana Díaz, and after my lesson, they decided to go to the hospital to visit Mami and Laura. I remember getting into Hermana Díaz's station wagon, a long, low car with extra space inside and wood trim on the outside.

Any other time, I would have been excited to ride in the station wagon, but not now. When we got to the hospital, I waited in the car with my aunt, and after what seemed like forever, Hermana Díaz returned. She was very somber and said that Laura would get better, but she was still very sick. My mother was going to stay with Laura.

Without any warning, my world had become a very dark place. I missed my mother and Laura. Even at five years old, I knew that an illness that required a hospital stay was serious. No one had explained to Mario and me what was wrong, but I couldn't forget Papá saying that some people had died. My sister might die, or if she lived, she might not get better for a long time. We were very scared.

Mario and I were not allowed to visit our mother and Laura. After a few days, we missed them so much that my father drove us to the hospital.

"Let's get out of the car," Papá said, pulling into a parking space. He showed us the window that was Laura's room, and Mario and I stared at it while Papá went inside. A few minutes later we saw Mami at the open window, leaning out through the curtains.

"There she is!" Mario exclaimed as my mother waved at us.

"Mami! Mami!" we called, though she was too far away to hear us. She blew us a kiss and then retreated back inside, leaving Mario and me fighting tears.

When my father came back outside, Mario and I were still looking up at the window where Mami had been. Papá must have seen how sad we were. "Let's go get an ice cream," he said, pointing to the Dairy Queen next to the hospital.

It was always a special treat for us to get ice cream. We left the car in the hospital parking lot and walked to the Dairy Queen's outside window to place our orders. Mario asked if he could have his ice cream cone dipped in chocolate, and to our surprise, Papá said yes, even though it cost extra.

I was fascinated with the swirl that the Dairy Queen worker put on the tip of the ice cream. As she dipped Mario's cone into a pot of melted chocolate, I wondered why the ice cream didn't melt too. After Papá paid, we sat on the outdoor bench, licking the sweet ice cream and talking about how Laura and my mother were doing.

"Laura would really like this ice cream—she loves chocolate," Mario said. We all agreed but said that Mami would have to feed the cone to her; otherwise, it would be too messy for her to eat. *If Laura and Mami were here,* I thought, *I'd give them my ice cream and not save even one bit for myself.*

But they weren't with us. I looked across the street at the hospital, at the window where I'd seen Mami. It was tiny and far away.

A few days later, after breakfast, Tía Angélica said, "Sylvia, tomorrow is Mami's birthday. Will you help me make a cake for her?"

I hadn't known we could have a birthday celebration

with Laura still in the hospital. "Let's make a strawberry cake," I said. "That's Mami's favorite." And Mami would have to come home to eat it, I thought.

Tía Angélica told me that Mami wouldn't leave Laura, even on her birthday. But Papá could take the cake to her as a surprise.

The next day was Saturday, so Papá didn't go to work. Right after breakfast, my aunt and I baked a strawberry cake with pink frosting and strawberries on top. It was the first cake I had ever made, and I was very proud. By the time Papá got up, the cake was ready.

"Your mother will like it," he told me. Instead of taking the entire cake to Mami at the hospital, he suggested taking her a big slice. But didn't he know that one slice wouldn't be enough?

"You have to take two pieces, one for Mami and one for Laura," I reminded him. My father only nodded, and I didn't understand why his eyes were filled with tears.

While my father ate his breakfast, Tía Angélica cut two big slices of cake. She put them on a plate and covered them with aluminum foil. The sticky frosting clung to the foil.

After he ate, my father got ready to leave for the hospital, but he forgot to take the cake with him. Luckily, I noticed before he had pulled out of the driveway. When he saw me running out the front door, he stopped the car. I gave him the plate with the cake, and he placed it carefully beside him on the passenger's seat. "Tell Mami I said Feliz cumpleaños, happy birthday," I told him, and he nodded.

As Papá drove away from the house, I sat on the front step and cried. I missed my mother so much, and now I wouldn't even see her eat her birthday cake. My aunt came outside and sat down next to me. She hugged me close as we watched my father turn the corner and drive out of sight. Laura was still sick, and Mami was with her, and there was nothing else we could do.

Tía Angélica

Mami

CHAPTER 4

She's Not the Same

I didn't see Mami at all on her birthday. That night, Papá came home from the hospital and told me how much she liked her cake. Tía Angélica served us big slices after dinner, and it was delicious. "Did Laura like it?" I asked Papá. But he didn't answer me, leaving the table instead.

I started to go after Papá, but Tía Angélica shook her head. "Laura's still too sick to eat," she said.

I thought about Mami eating her birthday cake while Laura lay in bed, not even hungry.

During the three long weeks that Laura was in the hospital, I saw my mother only a few times, when she came home to change her clothes. I thought the hospital rule that said Mario and I were too young to visit was stupid. My aunt sometimes took me to the hospital during the day, but I had to stay in the waiting area while she visited Mami and Laura. My aunt was always sad when she came back, but she would tell me that Laura was a little better.

Mami refused to leave my sister alone at the hospital, so if she wanted to make a visit home, someone else, usually Hermana Díaz, had to stay with Laura. Papá would pick up Hermana Díaz at the church, drive her to the hospital, then drive Mami home.

Mami always hugged Mario and me when she arrived for these brief visits, but she seemed so sad and worried. She would retreat to her bedroom to shower and change clothes, and I would hear her crying behind the closed door. I wanted to help, the way I'd helped to look after Laura before she was sick, but what could I do? I didn't even dare open the bedroom door.

Like my mother, my father was worried and upset, but he still had to go to his job, and every evening after work he would visit Mami and Laura in the hospital. During those long weeks, Tía Angélica kept us fed and clothed.

One Sunday while Laura was in the hospital, my

Abuelito Mario came to visit us. It had been a long time since we'd seen our grandfather at his home in El Paso. Now he was coming to our house. Before he arrived, my father was waiting outside, looking up and down the street, checking his watch every few minutes. I had never seen him so nervous and apprehensive.

Finally, a car pulled up, and my grandfather and another man got out. My abuelito didn't like to drive, so a friend had brought him to our house. Papá invited Abuelito Mario and his friend inside, but his father shook his head. He was snappily dressed, and he even was wearing a fedora.

Tía Angélica had made the living room look festive, with pretty lace doilies on the backs of the sofa and chairs. When my grandfather wouldn't come into the house, she brought cookies, coffee, and a fruit drink outside on a tray, and Mario and I helped ourselves to the cookies.

Usually when we had visitors, they stayed for a long time, talking with the grownups, eating and telling stories. My brother and I had been eager to show our grandfather our bedrooms and the yard, but after just a few minutes,

Abuelito said it was time to visit my mother and Laura at the hospital.

Before he left, Abuelito Mario gruffly reminded my brother, his namesake, to do well in school. I was a little scared of him, but I hugged him goodbye, and like a flash, he was gone, taking my father with him.

Mario and I helped my aunt carry the dishes back to the kitchen. "I wanted to show him my model planes," Mario said.

"Why was Abuelito's visit so short?" I asked my aunt.

"He wanted to see Laura and Mami, and maybe he was in a hurry to get back to El Paso," said Tía Angélica. Later, she said he might have been worried that he would get sick like Laura did, but if that were true, then why did he visit her in the hospital?

I was sorry that my grandfather hadn't stayed longer and disappointed that he had not spent more time with Mario and me. It was clear that my father idolized his father, and Abuelito Mario was a smart man and usually seemed to care for us when we were around him. But unlike my grandmothers, who were part of our extended family, my grandfather remained more like a visitor. That single trip was the only time he ever traveled the forty-five miles to Las Cruces to see his oldest son or daughter and their families. After that, if we wanted to see him, we had to visit him in El Paso.

One evening, several days after my abuelito's visit, my father announced, "Mami and Laura will be home tomorrow."

"Is Laura all well again?" I asked.

Papá didn't answer me for a minute. "She's starting to get better," he finally said. "You and Mario will have to help her."

Word spread up and down Griggs Street, and a few people arrived with food for our family. Mami had given away Laura's crib several months earlier, but when the neighbor who had it heard that Laura was coming home, she returned it. I made sure that Cucá was waiting in the crib.

The next day was Saturday. After breakfast, my father drove to the hospital and brought our mother and little sister home. He carried Laura into the house and laid her in her crib while my mother drew the shades in every room. She hung towels over the shades in our bedroom to make sure that no light came in. At first, Laura was asleep, but even when she woke up, she didn't seem to notice us.

The hospital had given Laura a pair of cheap plastic sunglasses to protect her eyes. "Laura," I called softly, trying to see behind the glasses. "Laura-ca-louda, Laura-ca-louda." But she looked straight past me as if I weren't there, the way she had on the day she'd gotten sick. Still, I thought, at least she wasn't burning hot now like she had been then.

In a sad voice, Mami explained that Laura's vision had been affected by the illness.

"Will she get better?" I asked her.

Mami said she didn't know. It was too soon to tell if Laura would ever see again.

Now the shades were always drawn, and our joyful home was dark and somber. Our mother no longer sang, no longer twirled us around the kitchen to the music on the radio. She was too sad to play with me or chatter while she cooked or cleaned. After Mario went to school in the mornings, I didn't know what to do. The house was too quiet, and after one attempt, I had stopped going to Hermana Díaz for lessons while my sister was in the hospital.

I didn't realize then that some of my mother's friends refused to visit us because they were afraid of catching Laura's illness. We'd see them at church, but they wouldn't come over to say hello. When Mami told Papá after church that not everyone would speak to us, he'd just shake his head.

Before Laura got sick, it was my job to look after her while Mami washed the dishes and cleaned the house. Now, my mother was ever vigilant, moving Laura's crib to whatever room she was in, never letting her out of her sight.

I'd peer over the side of the crib and talk to Laura, but she wasn't interested in me or in the things we used to do. I couldn't even see her eyes behind her dark glasses. Many times, Mami would leave the room in tears because her daughter didn't seem to recognize her. She did that only if Tía Angélica was there, though. Mami did not leave Laura alone with me, the way she had before.

I knew Laura couldn't see, but I had trouble imagining what that was like. I would walk around with my eyes closed, but I'd always bump into a wall or chair. My eyes would pop open, and right away, I could see again. Laura didn't seem to notice if I came into the room, didn't look at me until I said her name. And even when I spoke, she didn't always notice.

One day, Mami said, "Laura" as she fed her a spoonful of mashed bananas, and Laura looked at her, her eyes wide.

"Laura," I repeated, and my sister turned her head in my direction. Could she see me, or was she just responding to my voice? It was hard to tell, but I thought she met my eyes.

It took a little time before we were sure, but soon I could hold a doll out to Laura without saying anything, and she would reach for it. Now we knew she wasn't blind.

Even after Laura could see again, she was still so quiet. She would clutch her doll and stare at me without saying anything. She had stopped chattering in English and Spanish, stopped running after Mario and me. My little sister couldn't even walk anymore. Instead, she'd sit on the floor in her diaper and slowly pull herself forward with her legs and ankles.

Every day in the living room, Mami and Tía Angélica would spend hours singing and talking to Laura as they moved her arms and legs, hoping this would help her do the things she had done before she was sick.

Whenever Mami left the room, Tía Angélica stepped right in, crouching behind Laura and gently lifting her to her feet, encouraging her to walk. My aunt would turn on the radio and sing to Laura as they circled the wooden floor, Tía Angélica holding Laura upright and moving her little legs. "Sing and don't cry, lovely sky." Tía Angélica would sing her love songs, such as "Cielito lindo," and sometimes I'd sing too.

Over many long months, Laura began to walk and talk again, but she had changed. She still loved being around people, but she struggled to connect with them, to understand what they were saying. During these early months, she would hold Cucá tightly and stare at us, as if trying to figure out what was wrong. Mario and I would dance and sing in front of Laura's crib, hoping to get her to respond. Before she was sick, she loved to stand up, holding the side rail, watching us and laughing. Now, no matter what we did, she just lay quietly.

With Laura home from the hospital, my father returned to his routines: his job and his visits to the library, to his sister and mother across town, and to his father in El

Paso. As far as he was concerned, his little girl had survived a terrible sickness and was on her way to recovery.

But Papá no longer went to church. Before Laura got sick, Papá had been a lay minister and leader of our church choir. After Laura's illness, he felt betrayed that so many members of the congregation, instead of rallying around our family, stayed away from our home for fear of catching meningitis. He never really explained why he quit going to church, but he never went back. Even later, when I was older, I never knew if it was because he'd been bothered by the behavior of other members of our church, or if his faith itself was shaken by Laura's illness. He simply never talked about such things.

One friend who visited faithfully was Hermana Díaz. During her recovery, Laura had to take a lot of medicine, and she would cry and resist every time. When no one else could get her to eat and swallow her medicine, Hermana Díaz was able to coax her with a blend of kindness and firmness. For the first time, I saw how my teacher's strictness—and her generous heart—could be helpful. After several weeks, I was relieved when Mami let me resume my lessons with her. With all that had happened, my mother had forgotten for a time that Hermana Díaz was teaching me. I was so happy to be once again learning my letters and numbers in English in the little classroom inside the church.

Though our family and most of our friends wished to make things easier for us, my mother remained very sad for a long time. She blamed herself for Laura's illness and in some ways felt it was a form of God's punishment, even though she knew that others had gotten sick too and that the illness was caused by a microscopic organism. She knew those things, but she still couldn't help blaming herself.

Laura had been the one of us whose personality most resembled my mother's. Over time, it became clear that her illness had permanently affected her brain. The little girl who loved to learn, to dance, to run after the neighborhood children, to read books and chatter endlessly, was different now.

Mami was the first to realize that Laura would not fully recover, and she was frustrated that my father didn't seem to understand. "No entiendes. Ella está cambiada," she would tell Papá. *You don't get it. She is changed.* As far as Mami was concerned, she had lost her youngest child, almost as if

Laura had died from her illness. In the Mexican way of not wanting bad news to be true, she treated Laura as normally as possible, but Mami was inconsolable.

As for my father, he just kept going to work. With a family to support, what else could he do?

Even while she remained grief stricken, my mother began to take action. She reasoned that if she had been able to drive on the day Laura became ill, she could have gotten to the hospital more quickly.

Earlier, my father had resisted letting my mother learn how to drive and become more independent. At the time, it was unusual for women in our community to drive, and as the head of our household, Papá felt that it was natural that he would be the only driver in our family.

One night after dinner, with steel in her voice, Mami informed Papá that she would be taking lessons to get her driver's license. "Then, I will be using the car during the day when you are at work," she said.

I had never heard my mother speak in such a tone. My father protested, but Mami had thought of every possible objection. Since we had only one car, she told my father that she would get up early and drive him to the bus that took employees to the missile range. She would use the family car during the day and pick him up in the evening.

In the end, Papá didn't forbid Mami to take driving lessons. "Driving is harder than it looks," he warned her. My mother didn't answer him — but we all knew she didn't have to. Mami had gotten what she wanted, and now it was up to her to show Papá that she could learn to drive the car.

My mother had hired someone to teach her how to drive while my father was at work. The next day after lunch, a car arrived at our home, and as Tía Angélica, Laura, and I watched, the driving teacher moved to the passenger's seat, and Mami climbed behind the wheel. Slowly and carefully, she drove away, returning an hour later looking tired but triumphant.

Soon Mami passed the test and came home with her driver's license. She was still sad about Laura, so she didn't celebrate the achievement with her former exuberance. She acted like this was something she had to do, so she did it.

I think my father had not believed she would really go through with it. But early the next morning, Mami was ready to drive Papá to the checkpoint where he could catch the bus to the White Sands Missile Range. She made sure he was up early, too.

Even as a child I could see that things had changed between my parents. Instead of their former playful small talk, there was awkward silence. They were both sad, but they didn't seem to know how to be sad together. I wanted them to be happy again, to laugh and joke with each other—and with us. I wouldn't understand for a long time that Laura's illness had altered my parents' relationship, and things never would go back to the way they had been before.

My mother looked around at the dirt streets surrounding our home, at the tiny, rundown houses, at the cramped yards and the feral dogs. She knew that the meningitis outbreak had been confined to our neighborhood. If there was another epidemic, she was certain it would begin here too. And while the city did little to protect the people who lived on Griggs Street, she would protect her family. Even though she loved our community, Mami made up her mind: it might take her some time to find us a new home, but we would have to live somewhere else.

Laura, age three, after she recovered her sight

CHAPTER 5

A Head Start and
a Library Card

In the long months after Laura came home from the hospital, my mother continued to be very sad. I would hold Laura and help take care of her, but she didn't play the way she had before. Even though she wasn't sick anymore, she spent most of her time sitting quietly, holding her doll. She watched me and Mario, but she didn't try to play with us, didn't imitate everything we did. She wouldn't repeat the words I said or try to sing along with Mami. Worse than that was the way Mami acted—distracted and uninterested in me, in our community, in other people.

I wished that I could go to school with Mario to escape our too-quiet house.

Slowly, Laura had regained her eyesight, and over many months, she began to play. One day I put on a record, and she started to move around to the music. "¡Laura está bailando!" I called to my mother. *Laura is dancing!*

Mami smiled at the sight, but she wasn't as excited as I thought she would be. Still, Laura's progress filled me with hope. It was a long time before I saw that she could no longer learn new things the way she had in the past. Instead of chattering and imitating me and Mario, she lagged behind other children her age, walking unsteadily when they ran, giving one-word answers when other toddlers spoke in full sentences. Her life now would be very different than if she hadn't gotten sick.

My mother understood this already, and that's why she was so sad. But I was still only five years old, and I kept hoping that one day we would all wake up and things would be as they were before, with our bright, busy little sister and our happy parents — and a singing Mami. Every night for years, I prayed that in the morning Laura would wake up to her old self and our family would be happy again.

In the meantime, Mario went to school every day and I stayed home. As he progressed through first and then second grade, he brought home harder books to read. He told stories about his teachers and the friends he was making in school.

By now, my lessons with Hermana Díaz were the highlight of my days. I loved walking through the door of our makeshift classroom and sitting down to an hour of sounding out words, doing simple addition, and practicing my handwriting. Best of all, I liked speaking to Hermana Díaz in English, having her ask me a question and knowing the right words to answer her.

Still, while I had come to love my teacher, and I knew she cared about me, I couldn't wait until August, when I would start first grade at Bradley Elementary School. I was in a hurry to catch up to Mario and excited to learn new things.

One spring day, my brother brought home a piece of paper. His second-grade teacher said the paper had information about a way for children my age to go to school, even before they were old enough for first grade. Mario couldn't tell Mami anything more, and the paper was printed in English, so my mother had to ask a neighbor what it said.

The neighbor told Mami it was about a pilot program called Head Start. The program was for children like me, who were almost old enough for school. It would take place in the summer at Bradley Elementary School and would include meals, medical checkups, and lessons to prepare us for first grade, all of it free.

After our neighbor translated the paper, she told Mami not to enroll me in Head Start. She said we didn't know enough about it, and besides, it was only for kids from poor families. The meningitis outbreak had happened shortly after children from our neighborhood had been given a sugar cube with a few drops of medicine on it. The medicine was called a "polio vaccine." Polio was a terrible disease that attacked many children in those days. The polio vaccine was new, and no one was sure how well it would work.

No one could say why the meningitis outbreak had happened only in our part of Las Cruces, but the result was a general suspicion of government programs. Who knew if Head Start would really help us? It was only gradually over the years that people in our neighborhood realized that the polio vaccine had worked — there were no new cases of that terrible disease — but the suspicion remained.

This neighbor wasn't the only person we knew who was wary of Head Start. My mother soon learned that most of our neighbors would not enroll their children.

But Mami was thinking about the long, hot summer with all three of her children home every day. She thought this program seemed almost too good to be true. Without telling anyone except Hermana Díaz, she decided to enroll me.

I loved my early-morning time with my mother, when she would braid my hair and I had her all to myself. One day, while she was brushing my hair in front of the mirror in her bedroom, Mami asked me if I would like to go to a new program at Mario's school. She said it wasn't for Mario — he would stay home with Laura. It would be just me going to school that summer.

School in the summer! I didn't even have to wait for August to go to Bradley Elementary School. In the mirror, I could see myself grinning, and Mami couldn't help smiling back at me.

On the first day of Head Start, I walked hand in hand

with my mother as she carried Laura, crossing the sandy lots filled with sagebrush and tumbleweeds, on the way to Mario's school — but now it was my school too.

In the lobby of the school, I saw other mothers with children who looked about my age, all sitting in chairs and talking quietly in Spanish. The children were wearing their best clothes, as if they were in church — the girls in pretty dresses, their hair braided neatly, and the boys in pressed pants and button-down shirts. My mother found a lady named Mrs. Davenport, who seemed to be in charge.

I couldn't help staring. Mrs. Davenport seemed different from any woman I knew. Unlike Mami and the other mothers who waited with their children, she had fair skin and light brown hair in a style I'd seen on television — she was Anglo. She looked elegant to me, like Jacqueline Kennedy, the wife of President Kennedy. She was taller than my mother and wore a sleeveless, close-fitting dress with a belt.

Even though Mrs. Davenport didn't speak Spanish, my mother was able to tell her in broken English that I was her daughter and I was there to enroll in Head Start. Mrs. Davenport bent down to gaze at me with the bluest eyes I had ever seen.

"What is your name?" Mrs. Davenport asked me. I was proud that I knew the answer.

"Sylvia Elia Acevedo Monge," I answered confidently.

Mrs. Davenport shook her head. "No, that is too many names," she said. Confused, I glanced at my mother. I could tell she was also puzzled when she repeated my answer: "Sylvia Elia Acevedo Monge."

Mrs. Davenport asked my father's last name and my mother answered, "Acevedo."

Mrs. Davenport turned to me. "Then your name is Sylvia Acevedo," she said. I looked at her, not knowing what to say. I felt crushed, as if a part of me had been wadded up and discarded along with the two names that I wasn't allowed to use. Elia was my middle name and Monge was my mother's last name, and I was proud of them both.

Mrs. Davenport didn't even notice how I was feeling. She took us to a table and introduced us to the lady sitting there. My mother sat down with Laura on her lap, and the other lady helped her fill out some papers as I held tightly to Mami's free hand. I looked around at the other mothers and children who were sitting and waiting.

Then Mrs. Davenport called out to the children to

follow her. When everyone in the room stood up, she smiled and shook her head. "No, only the children," she said. But none of the mothers would let their children go. At last she took all of us, mothers and children, to the classroom.

When Mrs. Davenport opened the door, I gasped. Inside was a classroom like something I thought existed only on television. It was a whole room filled with toys, mats, books, easels, and art supplies, all in bright colors. Oh my, it was wonderful.

Now all of the children were fidgeting, as eager as I was to go inside. I waved goodbye to my mother and sister, barely noticing when they left along with the other mothers and babies and younger children who weren't old enough for Head Start. I was too busy exploring, picking up the new toys, the crayons and paper, the bright books.

After a few minutes, Mrs. Davenport had us sit down on the rug. Using a mixture of English and gestures, she told us that she would call our names and we would have to say "Here." When it was my turn, Mrs. Davenport called out, "Sylvia Acevedo!"

I answered "Here" out loud, just as she had told us to,

but inside my head, I was reciting the rest of my name to myself: *Sylvia Elia Acevedo Monge.*

Even though I wasn't allowed to use my full name, I had a good first day at Head Start. We colored a picture: a big circle, and our teacher taught us how to add other circles to it—a head, arms, and legs—to make it into a person We could use any color crayon we wanted, and I chose red. Mrs. Davenport taught us the alphabet song, and I was proud that I already knew all the letters. She read a book to us in English with lots of pictures, and I understood most of the words. We played with the toys, and we went outside and ran around in a yard.

At home that night, I asked my father why I couldn't use my full name at school. He explained that things were different in the United States, and I would soon understand that it wasn't just English that I was going to learn, but also a new way of life.

Papá's answer confused me. In spite of what I had learned from Hermana Díaz, I was still too little to understand that even though we lived in a neighborhood made up of families like ours, who visited relatives across the border or had other strong ties to Mexico, we did live in the United

States. I loved our close-knit family here in Las Cruces, including Tía Angélica and the Barbas, and our neighborhood and cultural traditions. I loved my Abuelito Mario in El Paso, Texas, and my Abuelita Leonor in Mexico. I didn't mind learning to read and speak English, but I didn't want anything else about our lives to change.

Even though I didn't like what Mrs. Davenport had done to my name, I soon came to adore my new teacher. She greeted every child with a smile and knew all our names by the second day. Like Mami, she loved to sing, and she taught us new songs in English. As for my name, I had learned that in the United States, I was Sylvia Acevedo. But when I traveled to Mexico, I embraced my full name, Sylvia Elia Acevedo Monge.

Thanks to Hermana Díaz, I was one of the few children in my Head Start class who understood any English at all. Mrs. Davenport quickly realized that I already knew the alphabet and my colors and that I recognized common shapes, like circles, triangles, and squares. All of this was usually taught in kindergarten, but with no kindergarten at Bradley Elementary School in those days, we would start first grade in the fall and be expected to have these skills.

While I spoke English better than most of the other children and could even read a few words, I wasn't too interested in arts and crafts — and I wasn't too good at them either. I wasn't like my brother, Mario, who loved to draw and paint. I never understood how he could just sit there with his model planes or drawings, spending so much time on the tiniest details. I preferred to read or play outside, not to be stuck inside doing arts and crafts.

On the Friday of our first week at Head Start, Mrs. Davenport announced that we'd have show-and-tell after lunch, and everyone could show off the projects they'd created with crayons, scissors, and glue. When it was my turn, I shook my head. I was a little envious of the students who proudly shared their work, but I didn't think any of my projects were special enough to share with the others.

Afterward, Mrs. Davenport took me aside. "Sylvia, next Friday, when we're doing show-and-tell, I want *you* to talk about a book," she said. Then she challenged me. "This is a book for first graders. I'd like you to read it and present it to the other children."

The book Mrs. Davenport gave me was about a girl named Jane and her brother, Dick. I had a brother! The children had a dog called Spot and a little sister, Sally. Mario and I had had a dog named Manchas, which is Spanish for "spot," and a little sister named Laura! I could read some of the book by myself, but I didn't understand all of the words.

When school was over, I took the book home and showed it to my mother. Mario was outside with his friends, so I couldn't get him to help me read it. My mother tried to help me, but some of the English words were unfamiliar to her. At last my father got home.

"Papá, Papá, Papá," I said, eager for his attention. Now I could ask him about the words I didn't understand. Papá was tired after a long day at work, but he answered my questions patiently while Mami cooked supper.

All week long, I practiced reading the book. My mother asked me to explain the story to her. When I answered her in Spanish, she said, "Dímelo en inglés." I had to tell her about the story in English.

I had to think about what my mother was asking. She didn't just want me to read the story aloud. Instead, I had to use my own words to describe in English what was happening. After I did that, she made me explain what I'd just said to her in Spanish. Then she made me tell her what I liked about the story.

This went on for a few days. Each afternoon, I presented the story to my mother, and I'd try to get to the point more quickly or tell her something new about it. I had to think of new English words to use and then translate them into Spanish.

By the time I had talked about the book to Mami's satisfaction, I had a lot of confidence reading and talking in English, and I wasn't nervous about speaking in front of the class. I was excited!

On Friday, our class sat in a circle on the rug. I kept my hands tightly around my book as my classmates held up their paper creations: crowns, paintings, and paper dolls. Then Mrs. Davenport called my name. Not scared at all, I told my classmates about Dick and Jane and their dog, Spot. I explained that "Spot" is the same as "Manchas" in Spanish. I talked about their sister, Sally, and the funny things they all did. I told them why I liked the book, and I read the first few pages aloud. Everyone laughed when I read about Spot running away with the teddy bear. Everyone was looking at me and listening to what I had to say—in English!

Before I went home that day, Mrs. Davenport gave me another book to read, with more stories about Dick and Jane and Sally. The next Friday, I talked about that book in show-and-tell. Each week after that, I took home another book, reading it and telling Mami all about it. Then I presented the book at show-and-tell. I was proud that I could read and talk in English in front of the class, just like Mrs. Davenport, and as time went on, I found I was never nervous when I had to speak in front of a group.

Now that I was learning to read complete books, I wanted to go to the library with Papá and my brother. Mario had been borrowing books on Papá's card, but Mrs. Davenport said children could get their own library cards and check out books themselves.

I thought Mami would like it if I had more books and learned to read faster, so one day I asked her if I could have my own library card.

To my surprise, Mami didn't say yes right away. She also didn't say no. Instead, Mami told me that I could have a library card—*if* I saved up five dollars. She explained that Papá was worried that if I somehow damaged any of the books I borrowed, the library would charge us to replace them. That's why I needed to have money saved up, in case I lost or damaged a book.

Mami didn't say anything about Mario, who was still checking out books on Papá's library card. She didn't say *he* needed to save any money. But I knew it would be a waste of time to ask her about this. Sometimes the rules were just different for me and Mario. In the meantime, I needed to save five dollars!

I already had a few coins in my bedroom. I showed them to Mami, asking her if this was enough money. "That's seventeen cents," she told me. "See, one dime is ten cents, a nickel is five cents, and you have two pennies. Ten plus five plus two is seventeen. One dollar is one hundred pennies." I hadn't known that.

That Saturday, Papá went shopping without us in Juárez and brought home a ceramic cat, black and shiny, with a slot in its back. "It's a bank," he explained. "You put your money in here, and before long, you'll have five dollars."

Papá didn't bring home a bank for Mario, only me. That puzzled me a little, because it was more usual that Mario got privileges that I didn't get. After all, he was the oldest—and a boy.

I carefully slid my coins into the bank, hearing them clink against the bottom. I couldn't see anything through the slot, but when I picked up the bank, I could hear the money jingling inside.

Suddenly, I had an eagle eye for loose change. Every time I went outdoors, I kept my gaze trained on the ground and was often rewarded with a penny, a nickel, and once even a quarter.

Not far away from our home was a tiendita, a little store that sold basic food and other items. Mami would sometimes send Mario or me there for milk or bread, and when she did, she'd let us buy candy or a soda with the change. Now I began to put aside some of the change for my bank. I'd buy a piece of penny candy, but I'd always hold back a coin or two.

I found money in other places as well. I would regularly feel under the sofa cushions, and if a coin had slipped out of Papá's pocket while he was watching TV, I'd seize it before he noticed. Whenever we passed a pay telephone, I'd race to stick my finger in the coin return slot, hoping to find a dime left there by the last person to make a call.

Now when I deposited coins into my bank, I could hear them hitting one another instead of the ceramic bottom. The bank felt heavy when I shook it, and I thought the cat looked pleased that I was feeding it so much money.

I felt very grown-up when I asked my mother for a dollar bill as my birthday present in August. She seemed surprised that I was asking for that and not a new toy, but she agreed. I remember folding the dollar carefully and pushing it through the slot. I shook the bank, but Mami said it was still not heavy enough. So I kept searching for coins to slide into the cat's back.

While I saved my money, I continued going to Head Start. And when Head Start ended, I started first grade at Bradley Elementary School.

Mario was in third grade, and he and his classmates sometimes made fun of the first graders. I didn't care. I was going to school, and because of Hermana Díaz and Mrs. Davenport, I was one of the best readers in my class. I loved everything about my school — the wide, cheerful hallways decorated with student work, the purposeful routines, the stories and songs we learned in English, and the games we played to help us learn our numbers and how to add and subtract.

My first-grade teacher was Mrs. Doggett. She had also been Mario's first-grade teacher, so I knew she was nice and that she'd told my brother he was very smart. I wanted to do well in her class so she could tell me I was smart, just like Mario.

Not all of the other first graders had been in my Head Start class, so there were many new students to meet. I was surprised that the mats, extra toys, and arts and crafts that we'd used in Head Start weren't available in our classroom. I missed Mrs. Davenport, but Mrs. Doggett was a good teacher too. She told me she remembered Mario.

Almost all of the students at Bradley Elementary were Catholic. Once a week after school, my Catholic friends would go to their catechism class at their church, and I would go directly home. I didn't mind getting to go home and play while my classmates went to catechism, but I knew that my family's Baptist religion made us different from most of our neighbors. I liked our church, but I wondered why we needed separate churches with different rules.

Meanwhile, I hadn't forgotten my goal of saving five dollars so I could get a library card. Every chance I had, I continued to pick up coins and drop them through the slot in my bank. After a while, when I added a penny, it clinked almost immediately against what seemed like an enormous pile of money. The bank was almost full.

I asked Mami if she thought I might have five dollars now.

Mami picked up the bank. "It's heavy," she said. She reminded me that to get the money out, I would have to break the bank. There was no other way. She covered the green Formica kitchen table with newspaper and gave me a hammer.

For the last time, I looked at my little black cat and stroked its shiny head. It seemed to look back at me. Maybe, I thought, the cat was saying that it had kept my money safe and now it was returning it to me. Then I raised the hammer and brought it down on the cat's back.

The bank shattered into pieces that flew all over our kitchen, revealing a pile of coins and my one-dollar bill. Surely there would be five dollars here.

Before I could count the money, though, Mami told me

I had to clean up. I had to put all the money aside on the table. Then she had me wrap the newspaper carefully around the plaster shards. The cat's head was intact, and I thought it was winking at me as I folded the newspaper and put it into the garbage. Next, I had to sweep the floor. Then, at last, I could count my money.

By now, I was very familiar with the different coins. I separated the pennies, nickels, dimes, and quarters, and I put them into stacks. I counted each one. I had more than eight dollars!

Mami brought out an old coin purse for me to put the money in. Next, she, Laura, and I walked to the downtown branch of the Doña Ana Bank.

Inside, we went right up to a teller's window. Mami told me to tell the lady standing there that I wanted to open a savings account, so I did. Then I poured the contents of the purse right onto the counter. The lady gave Mami some forms to fill out. She spoke Spanish, so Mami could understand her.

The lady handed me several paper sleeves in different sizes. She told me I had to roll up the coins in the sleeves before she could open the account. Mami and I counted stacks of ten pennies, and when I had five stacks, she showed me how to open up the sleeve marked for pennies and slip them inside. That was fifty cents. I had several rolls of pennies but only one roll of nickels and no complete rolls of dimes or quarters. I thought Mami was so smart when she pointed out that one stack was the wrong size. I counted again and saw she was right. She didn't make me feel bad for my mistake, though. Mami would never do that.

We soon had all the money rolled up and counted. Now I had to pass the coins and the dollar bill to the lady behind the window. I was worried about handing over my money, but the lady gave me a little book with my name typed inside. She showed me where it said how much money I had given her, right in the book, and she said I could bring in more any time and the bank would keep it safe. What's more, every few months, the bank would add a little bit of money to my account, which she called "interest." *Why?* I wondered. I didn't know that meant the bank was paying me to use my eight dollars while it looked after my money.

This bank was like a big version of my black cat bank, I thought, keeping my money safe. As we left, I looked around the lobby, just in case there were any black cats swishing their tails, but I didn't see a single one.

At last, we went to the library. Papá was at work, so Mami took me this time. We went home first to pick up Mario. Laura came too, even though she was too little to take out books.

Mami didn't even have her own library card back then. She told the lady behind the desk that she wanted library cards for Mario and me. The lady answered Mami in Spanish, but with an accent, so I thought she must speak English too. It didn't seem quite fair that I had saved up five dollars and Mario hadn't, but I didn't say anything. The lady sat down and tapped at her typewriter, and a minute later we each had our own wallet-size card with our name on it.

The lady stood up. "I'm the librarian," she said. She showed us into the children's room, a sunny alcove with shelves of brightly colored books, all of them in English. I saw magazines, too. Delighted, I pulled several books off the shelves and showed them to Mami.

"No," she said. "Take two. You have to save some for the other children."

I understood; that was fair. Besides, now that I had my library card, I could always come back for more.

Me, in first grade

CHAPTER 6

A Seat in the Back of the Classroom

E ven after two years, my mother still grieved over what had happened to Laura. My father didn't understand. His younger daughter was alive; we had not lost her. Every night when he got home from work, Laura ran to hug him. But my mother felt she had lost the child who was most like her, the toddler who had lit up the room with her spirit and energy. That little girl was gone.

As Mario and I moved up in school, reading and writing in English, we all saw that Mami had been right about the effects of Laura's illness. My sister had lost much of her ability to learn. In my mother's mind, the neighborhood that had been filled with laughter and joy now represented tragedy. If Mami spoke about these feelings, it was to mention the small, cluttered houses and yards and her worries that the neighborhood could be ripe for another epidemic of meningitis or some other disease.

Still haunted by her memories of the terrible day when Laura became ill, my mother had to get away to a place where our family could have a fresh start.

Mami wanted to explore neighborhoods that were farther away than our feet could take us. After she learned to drive, she started venturing out by car while Mario and I were in school. She didn't do it every day, but once in a while, she'd tell us about an expedition she'd made with Laura to a new part of Las Cruces. Sometimes Tía Angélica would go along too. We didn't think too much about this until Mami announced that she had found a new house for us.

Mami had mentioned several times that she had heard of a school that was supposed to be much better than Bradley Elementary. One evening, while we ate supper, she told us that she had been looking for a house near that school. Now she had found one within walking distance of it.

As Mami described the house—the pretty kitchen with new appliances, the spacious living room for the television, the yard—Papá looked straight ahead, and when he finally spoke, it was to ask Mario to pass him another tortilla.

We children sat silent. Would we be moving soon? Could we take all of our furniture and clothes? What if we didn't want to go to a new school? We didn't know the answers, and we were unsure whether to ask questions. Neither Papá nor Mami continued the conversation, but later, my mother and Tía Angélica took Laura and me to see the house. We couldn't go inside, but we peeked through the windows. It was much larger than our house, with a big backyard and a carport.

Over the next few days, it became clear that my father just didn't want to move. He avoided the subject whenever my mother brought it up.

Papá liked our neighborhood, and he didn't want the obligation of owning a house. We rented the one we lived in at the time, but to buy a house, Papá would have to borrow a lot of money from the bank to pay for it. Mami said this was called a mortgage. My father also knew owning a house came with a lot of chores. On the weekends, my uncle Sam sometimes recruited my father to help him around his own house, mowing the lawn or performing home maintenance. Papá much preferred the library to a Saturday spent cleaning the gutter or doing yardwork. He was not very good with his hands.

There was more to it than that, though. When Papá was growing up, the kids from Mexican families were shunted into vocational trades instead of being encouraged to go to college. When boys like him were told they were good with their hands, it sometimes meant they were being told they weren't smart enough for college. Papá was plenty smart, and he did go to college. Much later, I came to think that he took some pride in not being skillful at household chores.

All in all, Papá had plenty of reasons why he would rather rent a house, like the one we lived in now, than buy one. But my mother was not giving up, and the next time we saw Tía Alma and Uncle Sam, Mami brought up the subject of the new house.

Uncle Sam thought of himself as a big brother to my father. He had helped Papá get his new job, and they saw each other at work. Papá also visited him and Tía Alma every Sunday afternoon, sometimes after going to the library at New Mexico State University, where my father read chemical journals. When Uncle Sam said it was time for Papá to buy a house, Papá had to pay attention to his advice. Grudgingly, Papá agreed to purchase the house my mother had chosen, and he finally signed the loan documents, leaving Mami to do most of the packing and make all the arrangements, with help from Tía Angélica and Uncle Sam.

Now it was final. Despite its being the middle of the school year, we would be leaving our close-knit community where everything was nearby—our church, our school, and all our friends.

I couldn't help being happy to see Mami so excited, but I couldn't share her enthusiasm. I loved my school, and I hated saying goodbye to my teachers. On my last day at Bradley Elementary School, I didn't want anyone to see me cry, so instead of walking with my friends, I ran home as they called out to me, hot tears streaming down my face.

That day, the weather was unusually gray and cold for New Mexico. Before I went inside our old house on Griggs Street, I wiped my tears with my coat sleeve. By now, I knew my mother saw the move as a new beginning for our family. I didn't want to let her know how sad I was.

Inside, Mami and Tía Angélica had everything organized. Tía Angélica often stayed with us for extended visits, and she helped us with the move. My last day at the old school was a Friday, and by Saturday night, we were sleeping in our new house on Kay Lane, in beds made up with clean sheets.

I woke Sunday morning to see that my mother and Tía Angélica had stayed up most of the night, getting the house in order. My mother had breakfast ready for us, and we got to church on time, though it felt strange to drive there instead of walking a few short blocks.

Our friends at church greeted us as if we'd been away for a year, not just one day. Hermana Díaz asked me if I liked my new house. I didn't know what to tell her. My mother was happy to see her friends and invited them all to come visit. Since the new house was on the far side of town and most of my mother's friends did not drive, they told Mami that she would have to visit them. After the service, I looked longingly down the block, wishing we could go back to our old home.

Instead, that afternoon, I invented a game for Laura and me to put away our toys and clothes in our spacious new bedroom. My little sister thought moving to a new home was an adventure. She was happy just to play with me, to make a bed for her doll and to follow me around.

As I put the bedroom in order, I had to admit that it was nicer than the one we'd shared in our old house. The closet seemed enormous to me, and when we were done unpacking, there was still plenty of room left. There was even space for a desk.

By the time we'd lived on Kay Lane for a few days, I could see that our new neighborhood was completely different from everything I had ever known. For one thing, everyone spoke English — I had to get used to not hearing Spanish spoken except in our home.

The houses in this neighborhood were much newer than the ones in our old neighborhood. They were built on a former vineyard that had been planted with cotton during the Prohibition era in the 1920s, and for the first few years that we lived there, cotton plants would sprout in the yard. When we moved in, the front and backyards were just dirt, but soon grass and some weeds were growing — and they were the meanest and most persistent weeds in the world. Mami planted crabapple, willow, and mulberry trees, and she also tried to cultivate the grapevines that kept cropping up around the fences.

As for the house itself, it had two bathrooms, a kitchen with a new Formica counter, a screened-in back porch with sliding glass doors, a carport and driveway, and an air conditioner on the roof. We had never lived in a home with air conditioning before!

After we moved, we also had a telephone, which sat on its own little table in an alcove. Like all telephones in those days, ours had a long cord that plugged into the wall. We felt so sophisticated that we had our own phone number: 6-2939.

Most exciting for my mother was the real washing machine. It had been hard work for her to do the weekly laundry in our old house on Griggs Street. There, she'd struggled with an old-fashioned tub washer and its hand-cranked wringer.

In our new house, the washer was in the kitchen, and the laundry dried on clotheslines in the backyard. In the front yard were two small trees, a leafy mulberry and a palm tree. And all the streets were paved.

There were some things we didn't have, though. In our

old neighborhood, there were vendors who sold cantaloupes from horse-drawn carts, but we never saw them on Kay Lane. If we wanted a fresh cantaloupe, we'd have to go back to Griggs Street or to the store.

We'd have to go back to Griggs Street to see our friends, too. They seemed far away to me, and I decided I didn't like our new house, where we didn't know anyone. We didn't have Manchas, either. I still missed him sometimes.

On the Monday after we moved, a cold, gray day in the middle of January, Laura stayed home with Tía Angélica while my mother took my brother and me to enroll at our new elementary school. Mami had made us wear our best clothes, taking time that morning to iron everything, even our socks.

When my mother and father were first married, they'd had a difficult time finding an apartment, because many landlords in El Paso would not rent to "Mexicans," even though my father had been born in the United States. My mother always took extreme care with her own appearance and that of her children, not wanting anyone to say anything negative about us. In our new neighborhood, there were very few Mexican families. Even though we never heard anyone say anything unkind because of our heritage, Mami was always attentive to the way we — and our home — looked.

At Alameda Elementary School, the principal, Mr. McNeily, wore a formal dark-blue suit. He seemed very tall to me, much taller than Mami, who politely introduced herself and gave him our school records. Mami knew more English now, enough to carry on a basic conversation, but I could tell she felt intimidated.

"You're from Bradley." Mr. McNeily didn't exactly roll his eyes, but the way he looked at Mario and me left no doubt what he thought about my beloved elementary school and its loving, caring teachers. I wished that we'd never moved to a new home and that I were back in my old second-grade classroom at Bradley Elementary, not in the office of a new school with a principal who talked down to us.

My eyes filled with tears as he told us that Bradley Elementary School wasn't very good. I was so angry! I wanted to tell him that Bradley was a wonderful place, much better than his stupid school, but I knew better.

My mother, seeing my tears, pulled me in for a hug. "Todo va a estar bien, mija" — *Everything will be okay, dear daughter* — she said before she left the office. Now Mario and I were on our own.

Mr. McNeily showed Mario to a fourth-grade class-room, and my brother disappeared inside, giving me a quick, embarrassed wave. Then the principal brought me to another classroom. "She's from Bradley," he said to the teacher, and by now I knew this wasn't a good thing.

Mrs. Miller's classroom was crowded with forty seats, and every one was filled. I saw a few kids who looked Mexican, like me, but most of them were Anglo. While I stood waiting, the principal went into the hall and found another desk. He slid it into the last spot of the very back row, and I sat down.

It didn't take me long to learn that the classroom was organized by academic achievement, with the best student next to the teacher's desk and the worst student on the opposite side of the room in the back. As I took my seat in the last row, the boy in front of me turned around.

"Now you're the dumbest one in class," he said, and once again my eyes filled with tears. I hated that boy, and this class, and this school, and this neighborhood. But I had to sit there. There was nothing else I could do.

It turned out that Mr. McNeily had put me in a remedial class, for children who were far below grade level. He just assumed that because I was from Bradley, I was not a good student. Did he think that because most of the kids from Bradley were poor? Because we were Mexican? I didn't know the answer. I just knew he was wrong about my old school—and about me!

There was no remedial class in the fourth grade—in fact, there was only one fourth-grade class—so Mario wasn't disgraced the way I was. That first day, he came home and told us that when the teacher left the classroom, the kids went crazy, passing notes and throwing spitballs and paper airplanes. We were shocked. That never would have happened at Bradley!

By the end of my first day, I'd made up my mind that I would not stay the worst student in the worst second-grade class. I didn't know how I'd do it, but I'd find a way to move up.

My chance came that Friday, with the arrival of the *Weekly Reader.* I was familiar with this magazine from my old school. Mrs. Miller distributed our copies, and then, starting with the best student in class, she had everyone read a few sentences aloud. As she progressed through the room to the back of the classroom, the reading wasn't as strong, with students stumbling over words that I could read when I was in Head Start, before I started first grade.

Since I was in the very last seat, I was the last student to read. And when it was finally my turn, I read well. I remember it was a long article about the astronauts in the space program, and I knew every word.

I read until I'd finished the article. Then I closed the magazine and looked at Mrs. Miller. "That was very good, Sylvia," she said. "Stand up." Rearranging the other students, she immediately moved me to a desk in the middle of the classroom. I wasn't the worst student anymore! I'd moved halfway up the class in one day, just because I was a good reader. It was as if my first few days at the last desk in the last row had been erased from everyone's memory.

It was so strange to me, as if all of a sudden I was somebody different. I wasn't, of course. I was happy not to be the worst student in the second grade, but I still felt sorry for those children who'd had a hard time sounding out their words. Somehow, I didn't think it was their fault. Maybe they'd just never had the chance to attend Head Start, the way I had.

My class photo

CHAPTER 7

No One to Talk To

G lemboski, over here!"

"Stewart, you slowpoke!"

"Out of my way, Thompson!"

I swung on the monkey bars, my braids hitting the ground with a *thwap, thwap* on each upside-down loop, shouts from the baseball field rising over the playground noise. Every once in a while I'd hear "Acevedo!" and I'd know Mario was out there with the other boys.

After a few weeks in my new school, I was still startled to hear names like Radwanski, Burton, Schramm, Wallace, and Boudreau on the playground—kids whose families had come from all over Europe. At my old school, we sometimes spoke Spanish on the playground, and most of the children had last names like ours: Trujillo, Sánchez, García, González. Now I almost never heard Spanish words at school, as if Alameda Elementary School were in a different country from where my family had lived before.

Only the boys shouted one another's last names while throwing a ball or tearing around the field. The girls' voices were quieter, rarely rising above the din. But unlike at my old school, both girls and boys used the playground equipment. At Bradley, I'd sometimes skip rope or play hopscotch with the other girls, but they'd never join me on the monkey bars. I was always welcome to do what they were doing, but they had no interest in trying something new.

Now, at Alameda, I loved that I wasn't the only girl climbing the monkey bars. I'd watch the other girls, so agile and flexible, flinging themselves from one side of the metal bars to the other in just seconds. A few would even launch themselves off the top of a swing, which I could never get quite right—I always seemed to launch myself too late. I recognized a couple of the girls from other classes in my grade, but they never seemed to notice me. I was still the new kid here, and I felt very alone.

In those days, boys could wear jeans or overalls to school, but girls had to wear dresses or skirts unless the temperature was below freezing. When that happened, we were allowed to come to school in pants — as long as we wore a dress over them.

If the weather was good, I'd wear shorts under my dress so I could play on the swings and monkey bars without showing my underwear. I also liked to swing on a horizontal bar that was a few feet off the ground, my braids hitting the dirt surface of the playground each time I swung around.

When I got home, my mother would shake her head and say, "¡Tu pelo está sucio . . . otra vez!" — *Your hair is dirty again!* — because my head was so dusty.

Mami knew I wasn't going to stop running around. If my hair got dirty, that was okay with me. I'd smile at her, and she'd call me her machetona, her little tomboy. I'd glance around at the crowded living room with its familiar furniture, at my little sister looking up from her doll, waiting for me to play with her, and I'd sigh in relief. I was home.

I'd grab a homemade flour tortilla and slather butter on it, then roll it up like a flute. "Only one," Mami would say. "I don't want you spoiling your appetite." She'd hand Laura a petite tortilla that she had made just for her and tell us both to go outside and play.

Thanks to my mother and Tía Angélica's constant care, Laura was regaining her spark and enthusiasm for people. She could walk and run again, but she didn't say very much. She seemed especially puzzled when Mario or I spoke in English, and she was more comfortable speaking in Spanish. She loved looking at birds and listening to their songs. When someone mentioned school, though, Mami just looked sad. Laura wasn't old enough for school yet, but I could see that even a couple of years from now, she might have trouble learning in a first-grade classroom.

Still, she was my little sister, and we played together every day. Outside in the backyard, we'd make up stories with Laura's dolls, careful not to uproot the new grass. Mami had started an herb garden with mint and oregano and planted rosebushes. She took such special care with the roses that they didn't dare not bloom.

Some days Laura and I would use the hose to water

the plants in the backyard. Even in early spring, it was hot outside, so I didn't mind when she splashed me.

Soon Mami would come out to take the laundry down from the clotheslines. The air was so dry that after a couple of hours, the clothes were stiff as boards. I'd reach up and tug at a sheet or a pair of pants, and the clothespins would go flying. I wasn't tall enough to reach the smaller things, like our socks, so Mami had to help with those.

"Did you make a new friend today?" she'd ask me. "What did you learn in school?" I never knew how to answer her, so I'd look for clothespins on the ground until she changed the subject and remarked on how beautiful the Organ Mountains were in the distance. I knew Mami would be sad if I told her how much I still missed my old school, and I couldn't tell her that I didn't speak to the other girls in my class, not ever.

I knew Mami was puzzled that I hadn't made friends, but I couldn't talk about it. Even if I was more of a tomboy than the girls back in our old neighborhood, I'd known them as long as I could remember, and I felt accepted by them. Now I felt shy. I didn't know these new girls at Alameda

Elementary. With their loose blond hair and fair skin, most of them didn't look like my family.

In the cafeteria at lunch, I'd see girls from my class at a table, deep in conversation. After a few weeks, I knew their names: Cindy, Liz, Sarah, even another Sylvia. But that didn't mean I was going to sit with them or play with them at recess. Instead, I'd find an empty seat at another table and eat quickly by myself before going out to the playground, or I'd run home to share a sandwich with Mami and Laura.

Often when I arrived home, Mami would be sewing, maybe a new dress for Laura or me. I knew she wished I shared her interest in clothes and fashion, but she loved me even though I didn't care too much about those things. As far as I was concerned, the future everyone expected for girls—getting married and keeping house, sewing and cooking, taking care of children—was far away. In the meantime, I liked to ride my bike, run around, and play outside.

One place where I saw other girls like me was on television. In those days, Disney's programs, like *The Mickey*

Mouse Club after school and its Sunday-night shows, had as many tomboys as princesses. One Sunday, Disney broadcast *The Parent Trap* with Hayley Mills, a movie about twin girls who grow up apart but meet at summer camp. I was enthralled by their characters' daring escapades. My favorite shows were about girls who had adventures, who were allowed to do the same things as boys. But I didn't know any girls like that in real life.

In our culture, sons were valued over daughters. My father loved me, but he had different expectations for Mario and me. Mario got a library card without having to save a single penny, let alone five dollars, the way I had. Papá expected me to get good grades in school, but it was never with the same interest that he took in my brother. Papá never asked me what I wanted to be when I grew up, the way Mami did. I knew he expected me to get married, have children, and keep house, just like Mami. He even said so sometimes.

This made me mad, but it was just how things were. Besides, Mario was two years older than I was. He learned to read before I did, and a lot of other things, too. That didn't stop me from trying to catch up. I envied Mario. It was easier for boys to grow up and have adventures, I thought. I didn't know what to do about that, but over time I became ultracompetitive with my brother.

In the meantime, after we moved, Mario was better than I was at making friends. While I was playing by myself at recess and walking home alone after school, he'd found a whole group of new friends, boys who lived in our neighborhood.

One day after school, Mario told us, "These kids all think I know how to play softball like they do. Well, I don't."

But Mario's friends taught him how to play catch and swing a bat, so he could play softball with them. Mostly, though, they played army, either with toy guns and cardboard forts or with model airplanes and tanks they blew to pieces with firecrackers. The majority of his new friends were from Anglo families, because that was who lived in our neighborhood.

To help ease us into this new life, Mami adopted a puppy, a cocker spaniel–German shepherd mix, who soon became the king of the neighborhood. She and Mario named the dog Fito as a joke—a Spanish twist on the American Fido. I liked playing with Fito, but he was really Mario and Mami's dog.

I remained sad and fearful, still unsettled by the move. Every morning, I dawdled over my cereal at breakfast, begging Mami to let me watch the Captain Kangaroo show until almost the very end. I knew I could do that and get to school on time if I ran fast enough.

Normally, my mother would have teased me for my skittish behavior, but she left me alone. Even though she was happier in our new home, she too was still coping with all of the changes in our lives.

How could I explain what was bothering me when I didn't understand it myself? Part of it was school: at Bradley Elementary, the teachers told us what we needed to know. I had a good memory for facts, so I did well. At my new school, we had to work out more of the answers for ourselves. That wasn't as easy. Even though I thought I was doing well at school, I always worried that I wouldn't have the right answer and the teacher would move me back to the very last seat in the last row. If that were to happen, I didn't think I could stand the shame.

After school, I'd rush home and lock the door behind me, something I'd never done when we lived on Griggs Street. My brother and I used to fight, like all brothers and sisters. Occasionally, I would lock Mario out, usually by accident but sometimes on purpose, and he'd mash the doorbell until I let him in. "It's safe here," he'd tell me. "You don't have to lock the door!"

But I kept locking the door. I couldn't tell him why I had to; I just did. I felt safer at home, away from my new school and the blond girls who seemed nice but were still strangers. There were a lot of things I couldn't explain to anyone, but I felt as if I needed to protect us. Locking the door just seemed like the right thing to do.

Me, in third grade

CHAPTER 8

Learning to Pass the Scissors

As winter turned to spring, I still ate lunch by myself and spent recess alone. If someone had asked whether I was lonely, I would have said no, because I wouldn't have known what else to say. I never liked to talk about how I was feeling, especially when I was still confused by all the change in our lives. But except when the teacher called on me, I went through the long days without speaking. When the bell rang at the end of the school day, I hurried out of the classroom, not looking to see if anyone else might be going in the same direction as I was.

One spring day after school, I was nearly home when I

saw a girl, also named Sylvia, right around the corner from our new house. Sylvia Black was one of the smarter kids who sat near the teacher in our classroom. Today she was dressed in a brown uniform, one I'd seen on a few other girls. She hurried to catch up with me, so I reluctantly slowed down. Slightly out of breath, Sylvia said, "I didn't know you lived around here. I live on the other side of Alameda."

"What are you doing here?" I asked her. I hadn't seen her in the neighborhood before.

"Going to Brownies," she said. "It's Girl Scouts, but for girls our age. Do you want to come with me?" I'd never heard anything before about Brownies or Girl Scouts, but whatever they were, I wasn't interested.

"I don't know," I said, half hoping Sylvia might not wait for me. "Maybe. I might have to help my mother."

"That's okay," Sylvia said. "I'll wait while you ask your mom if you can go. You'll like it—it's fun," she added.

How does she know I'll have fun? I asked myself, sure that Brownies was for girls who already had friends of their own. Furthermore, I'd noticed that Sylvia didn't seem to have many close friends. I was not at all sure that I wanted to be friends with her—or anyone.

My mother was in the kitchen when I went inside, trying to figure out what to ask so she'd tell me I had to stay home. "You don't have to say yes, but this girl from school is going to a Brownies meeting or something. She said I could come, and she's waiting outside." My words came out in a rush. "It's okay if you say I can't go," I added, hoping Mami would say just that.

My mother smiled at me. Wiping her hands on her apron, she walked with me to the front door and waved to Sylvia. In Spanish, she asked me where the meeting was, and I translated the question for Sylvia, who recited the address in English. Satisfied with the answer, Mami said she'd see me after the meeting. Now I had no choice—I had to go.

From the moment I walked into the Brownies meeting, I could tell it was different from anything I'd ever experienced. The meeting was in a house near ours, but this house was bigger and it had a garage, not just a carport. Inside was a group of cheerful girls in brown uniforms and two women—troop leaders, Sylvia explained—who greeted me warmly and seemed very glad I was there.

The girls were all crowded around the kitchen counter,

drinking fruit juice and eating cookies. I recognized some of them from school. One or two girls said hi and I smiled back, just a little. Someone handed me a cup and told me to help myself. Then the leaders called us to start the meeting. We all went into the carpeted living room, and I saw that the furniture had been pushed back against the walls.

The leaders' names were Mrs. Provine and Mrs. Davenport, though this Mrs. Davenport was taller than my former Head Start teacher. I wondered if the two Mrs. Davenports knew each other. The girls sat down in a circle and Mrs. Provine said, "This is Sylvia Acevedo. Let's go around the circle and introduce ourselves." One by one, every girl said her name.

Next, each of them held up her right hand with two fingers in the air, and in unison they said, "I promise to do my best to love God and my country, to help other people every day, especially those at home." The troop leaders joined in too. I realized they were reciting a pledge of some sort, and everyone except me knew the words and what to expect. The girls were so organized and orderly. A few of them had a book called *Girl Scout Handbook* with an emblem printed on the blue-green cover. I learned later that there was a separate handbook for Brownies, but no one in that troop had it.

The Brownies were preparing for an upcoming nature outing in the park. Everyone seemed to take it for granted that I would join them. That afternoon, we were cutting fabric and newspapers into strips and weaving them into something called a sit-upon. I loved this idea: now we wouldn't have to sit directly on the ground, because we'd have our nice portable sit-upons. I knew my mother would appreciate them too, since she was always after me to keep my clothes clean. I was sorting through fabric strips and old newspapers, listening to the chatter around me, when the girl next to me asked for the scissors. Wanting to be helpful, I handed them to her eagerly, point first.

Suddenly, Mrs. Provine was at my side calling all the Brownies to attention. I looked up at her, puzzled. She asked two Brownies to stand up and gave one of them a pair of scissors. Then she asked the girl with the scissors to pass them to the other girl. Carefully, the girl holding the scissors put her hand around the closed blades. Next, she held out the pair to the other Brownie, handles first. She turned to me and said seriously, "That is the safe way to pass scissors."

The other girl added, "You also never run with scissors."

Mrs. Provine turned to me. "You see, Sylvia. This is the way Brownies pass scissors safely to others."

And I did see. At first I was embarrassed. I'd been singled out and told I was passing scissors the wrong way. But as the other girls went back to making their sit-upons, I saw that nobody was looking at me. Nobody was making fun of me or teasing me for being wrong.

I remember continuing to sort out the fabric strips for my sit-upon, thinking that I hadn't known there were rules about passing scissors. No one had ever told me about such a thing. Now I knew the rules, so I could do it safely too.

Suddenly, the crowded living room brightened, and I felt as if a weight had been lifted off my chest. I felt hopeful.

If these girls and their leaders cared so much about how to pass scissors, how much more would they care about other things? *Brownies and Girl Scouts make plans,* I thought. They make sit-upons so they don't get wet or dirty when they sit in the park, and they pass the scissors the *right* way. They care about how to do things correctly and safely, and they wanted to teach me these things too. And, I realized, that meant they cared about *me*.

Out of nowhere, I remembered the terrible day when Laura got sick and Mami had to beg for a ride to the hospital. I remembered how out of control everything had felt and how upset I was that there was nothing I could do to help. Now, almost for the first time since Laura's illness, I felt I had control, and with it, I felt an enormous sense of relief.

As I wove together the fabric strips I'd chosen, I knew I wanted to be a Brownie. I loved every minute of the meeting: the plans for an outdoor nature day, the practical sit-upons, the friendliness, and, more than anything, the sense of security and belonging to a wider world. I didn't even mind being told how to pass the scissors, because the Brownies could tell me how to do things the right way.

After the meeting, Sylvia asked if I wanted her to walk me home. "You can go on," I said. "I want to stay for a minute." Sylvia left, looking puzzled.

Then I waited until most of the other girls had gone.

"Did you want something, Sylvia?" asked Mrs. Provine, noticing me standing alone.

"That handbook," I said. "Can I borrow it? I promise I'll take care of it and give it back."

"You can have my older daughter's handbook," she told me. "She doesn't use it anymore. Just wait here while I find it." In a minute she was back. "You can keep it," she said, handing me the book. "No need to return it."

To end the meeting, we had sung a song about a great big Brownie smile, and now, as I hugged the *Girl Scout Handbook* tightly to my chest, I could feel that Brownie smile warming my cheeks all the way home. I thought about the upcoming expedition, when we'd be exploring nature. Maybe this was a way to find girls like those I'd seen on TV, girls like me, who wanted to have adventures!

That weekend, I read through the entire handbook, straightening out the dog-eared pages and erasing all the pencil marks. I had been mesmerized by the way the meeting had begun, when the girls and troop leaders recited the pledge together, but at the time, I couldn't take in all the words. Now I read them carefully.

The Girl Scout Promise was slightly different from the Brownie Promise we'd recited at the meeting. I reminded myself to get the words to the Brownie Promise at the next meeting, but for the time being, I would learn the promise that older Girl Scouts had to say.

"On my honor, I will try," the promise started. It continued: "To serve God and my country, to help people at all times, and to live by the Girl Scout Law."

I could promise, I thought.

The Girl Scout Law was longer. "A Girl Scout's honor is to be trusted," it began. That was the first of ten laws. "A Girl Scout is loyal," read the second law. Girl Scouts had a duty to be useful and to help others, to be a friend to all and a sister to every other Girl Scout. They were courteous and were friendly to animals. They obeyed orders and were cheerful, thrifty, and clean in thought, word, and deed.

I could try to be all of those things, I told myself. I stood in front of my bedroom mirror, practicing the two-finger salute and reciting the promise and the laws over and over until I could say the words from memory.

I also learned from the guide that the Brownies were

the Girl Scout division for girls my age, in second and third grades. At the end of third grade, we'd have a "flying up" ceremony and become Juniors, the Scouting division for girls in fourth, fifth, and sixth grades. Even older girls in junior high and high school could be members, as Cadettes and Seniors. I liked knowing that I could stay a Girl Scout for years and years, and I'd have a proper place no matter what age I was.

The Brownies met once a week after school, on Wednesdays, and I walked to the meetings with Sylvia and the other Brownies. After my fourth week, Mrs. Provine told me she had something for me. When all the girls were sitting in a circle, she came over and fastened a pin shaped like a trefoil to my blouse. It looked a little like a clover with three leaves. I'd noticed that all the other girls wore them on their uniforms. She told me that the pin's three leaves represented the three parts to the Brownie and Girl Scout Promises and that I was now officially a Brownie Girl Scout, just like all the other girls in the troop. I was so proud!

Mrs. Provine also told me that Brownie dues were one dollar, and I could bring the money whenever I wanted. One dollar for a whole year! My troop leader said that my money would help the Girl Scouts all over the country.

By now, I got a regular allowance of twenty-five cents every week. Back then, a quarter could buy two Cokes and a candy bar. A gallon of gasoline for my parents' car was twenty-nine cents. Whenever I saved up a dollar, I deposited it into my bank account downtown. I already had a few coins saved in my bedroom. As soon as I had a dollar, I brought it to the meeting.

Over the next weeks, I learned more about the Brownies from the troop leaders and the other girls. Brownies were discoverers. We were ready helpers.

Best of all, we were friend makers. I still felt shy sometimes, and I was still very quiet at school, even when another Brownie said hi to me, but I hoped some of these girls would be my friends.

The only thing keeping me from being a Brownie in every way was that I didn't have a uniform. Fortunately, my mother could see that the meetings were doing me a lot of good. She liked hearing me talk about the other girls and our plans, and she could see I was excited.

Even though Mami sewed most of our clothes to save

money, she decided to buy me a uniform. One Saturday, our entire family drove to the Popular, the big department store in El Paso, where I tried on the brown dress, the beanie, the belt, and the orange tie. When I saw my reflection in the mirror, I felt so special. I remembered something that Mrs. Davenport had told us: every time we saw a girl wearing the Brownie uniform, we knew she had made the exact same Brownie Promise we had.

To my surprise, my mother even bought me socks with the Brownie emblem on them! Sometimes it seemed that Mami could read my mind. I wouldn't have dared ask for the socks, but she knew I would love them.

I wouldn't let my parents put the bag with the uniform in the trunk of the car. On the drive back to Las Cruces, I kept the package on my lap.

As soon as we arrived home, I raced into my bedroom to change. Mami followed with her sewing kit, measuring to make sure the skirt was the right length. She helped me adjust the belt and fasten my trefoil pin to the uniform, but when I handed her the tie, she said I'd have to ask my father. "He can show you how to knot the tie," Mami said.

Dressed in my uniform, I pestered Papá, who was watching TV in the living room. "Papá, Papá, Papá!" I said, making my voice a little louder each time, until my father got up from the sofa and took me into the green bathroom. He put down the toilet seat cover and told me to stand on it. Then he swung open the door to the medicine cabinet and stood behind me so I could see both of us in the mirror. Step by step, watching our actions reflected in the mirror, he taught me how to tie the orange Brownie tie.

I thought we would be done once I'd knotted the tie to my father's satisfaction, but I was wrong. My father had been a commissioned officer in the United States Army, and he took my uniform seriously. He told me I had to be worthy of it, to keep it looking sharp. Was I ready to honor this uniform?

In answer, I held up my hand in the two-fingered Girl Scout salute. "On my honor," I told my father. And I meant it.

The night before the next Brownie meeting, I laid out the entire uniform on my bed to make sure I had everything. That weekend, I had washed my white tennis shoes and laces by hand so they'd look as good as my new uniform. My mother was shocked — she'd never seen me take such an interest in my clothing before.

The next morning, after Mami brushed and braided my hair, she surprised me with a new headband that matched my Brownie uniform. Sitting in front of the vanity in my parents' bedroom, seeing both of our reflections in the mirror, I was absolutely giddy with excitement. I beamed and my mother smiled back at me, her mirrored face reflecting happiness in a way that had been rare since Laura's illness.

At breakfast, I ignored my brother's teasing about my new uniform. By now, I knew he was just trying to get me to react. Walking to school, I felt so proud, and I was careful not to get dirty during recess. This was one day when my braids would not get dusty, I thought, reaching up to touch my headband.

At lunch in the cafeteria, other Brownies noticed me in my new uniform and waved to me. Proudly, I sat down to eat with them. Liz and Cindy were there, and another girl from my class. There were a few girls from other classes who were also members of my troop. I saw Sylvia Black sitting at another table with a few other girls in Brownie uniforms. I liked the way the uniform linked me to all the other Brownies and to the older girls in their Girl Scout uniforms. Wearing the uniform felt like a way to make friends — and it was.

As soon as I walked into the meeting that afternoon, my troop leaders noticed what I was wearing. "You look very nice in your new uniform," said Mrs. Provine. I could feel myself beaming with pride as I took my place in the circle of girls and got ready to say the Girl Scout Promise. In every way now, I was a real Brownie.

Me in my uniform!

CHAPTER 9

Christmas Traditions

Unlike most girls I knew, I had only one doll, a baby boy named Óscar, a Christmas gift from my grandmother. Óscar had once had a full head of dark hair, but that was before Mario used his barber skills on him. After that he was bald, but I didn't mind.

I never played with Óscar much, even when I was little, but at Christmastime, I needed him. That was because every year, Óscar had to be the Baby Jesus while I was Mary.

It started when I was in third grade, the fall after we moved to our new home and I joined the Brownies. One day, my music teacher told us we were going to audition for parts in the Christmas pageant. "I want you each to sing a song," she said. "Then we'll see who will sing which parts in the choir."

I liked singing. At home, Mami loved to sing, and she had a beautiful voice. Papá liked to sing too, but he seldom did. I thought my voice was just as nice as anyone else's in my family.

That day in school, we all lined up on the side of the classroom, and one by one, the teacher had us sing a verse of any song we liked. When it was my turn, I started to sing, and the teacher asked me to try again, a little lower. So I started again at the beginning, a little lower and a little louder.

When I finished, the teacher looked at me. "We're going to have a special part for you," she said.

I didn't know what that meant until she started lining up the class in rows, boys in the back and girls in the front. They would be the choir, she explained. After she finished, I stood alone with four boys. She told us we were to be the stable scene. All we had to do was pretend we were with the Baby Jesus in the stable. I could hold my doll and be Mary, and one of the boys would be Joseph. The other boys were the three wise men. As long as we didn't sing, she would be happy with our performance.

Mami knew my singing voice wasn't as good as hers, and she thought my teacher had come up with a clever solution. My mother was happy for me to be Mary, and she even made me a costume. The night of the pageant, I sat onstage, draped in my robes, holding Óscar, while the choir sang. I enjoyed listening to the Christmas songs, and every once in a while I'd look down at Óscar, daydreaming about the special holiday food we would have for Christmas.

The next year, my school didn't have a Christmas pageant, so I wasn't singled out. We sang Christmas carols at a schoolwide assembly, and I sat with my class. But Mami thought I should still be Mary. That year, and for many years afterward, I played Mary in our church's Christmas Cantada.

The Christmas Cantada—the musical performance of the Christmas story—was the most important event in Mami's year, and she spent much of the fall at the church, helping with the elaborate preparations for the performance and the reception afterward.

She usually sang solos at the Cantada too. She would

be very nervous beforehand, but she loved it. I had to help more around the house when she was busy at the church, especially cleaning up dinner after I'd finished my homework.

I didn't care, though. My mother sang only when she was happy. When she was busy with the Cantada and practicing her solos, it felt like all was right with the world.

On the morning of the Cantada, Mami was a whirlwind, getting us ready to go over to the church. As soon as the performance was done, we invaded the social hall, which was filled with wonderful food. Kids were buzzing all around, enjoying the feast and the energy of Christmas. Now the holiday was just around the corner.

After the Cantada, my mother focused on our family's holiday celebration, starting with a shopping trip in El Paso.

Trips to El Paso were fun because we got to experience the big city, both in El Paso, Texas, and in Juárez, Mexico, right across the border. We rarely went shopping as a family, and most of my experience of stores was in the small markets in Las Cruces, where Mami watched every penny. With Christmas coming, we would spend the whole day shopping.

The El Paso stores had goods that we never saw in Las Cruces: shiny appliances, furniture, and a wide selection of clothing. Mami loved to walk up and down on the sidewalks, looking through the store windows at the latest fashions and shoes.

We had a Woolworths in Las Cruces, but the one in downtown El Paso was huge by comparison. It sold all sorts of toys, and it was also where Mami bought the fabric and patterns to make our clothes. Another El Paso store was S. H. Kress, which had rotisserie chickens spinning in the window. They looked delicious, but at fifty-nine cents each, Mami said they were outrageously expensive.

Our big shopping trip usually started at the Popular, a department store so large it had elevators. There were several floors and a bookstore that took up the entire mezzanine. It was almost as big as the entire children's book section at our library in Las Cruces.

Once inside, Mami found it easy to distract us so she could shop for our presents. "Sylvia, take Laura to look at the dolls," she'd say, and we'd never suspect she was heading for the floor that sold books. Or she'd send us to the book section so she could buy toys. We were so wide-eyed that she could easily do all the shopping, and put the gifts in the trunk of the car, with us none the wiser. We would return to Las Cruces late at night, happy and spent, never dreaming our Christmas presents were returning with us.

Christmas wasn't just about presents or the Cantada. There were special foods, too. With her shopping done, my mother spent hours making the traditional Mexican foods of the season: tamales, pumpkin empanadas, crispy buñuelos, and bizcochos, which were holiday cookies. Mami also loved to try making new foods, especially during the holidays.

One year at Christmas, my mother taught herself to make fancy French-style cookies with just a light coating of chocolate on one side. My father told Mami she must have forgotten to coat the entire cookie! Indignantly, my mother replied that it was supposed to be that way. I was proud to have a mother who'd learned how to make cookies from faraway France. Years later, when I went to France, I looked for those cookies and was delighted to see them in bakeries.

In the weeks before Christmas, Mami filled tins with cookies and holiday treats, including one of my favorites: cinnamon rolls with walnuts and pecans. Whenever a tin was opened, we would devour the whole thing, leaving nothing for later. So my mother would hide a few tins from us around the kitchen and pantry. She would wait until we had opened all our gifts on Christmas morning, and then she would surprise us with cinnamon rolls.

On Christmas Eve, my mother would wake me early in the morning to help make tamales. Mami's sisters and friends would come over to help with the "tamalada"—the tamale-making party. Together, we would assemble more than twelve dozen tamales, including at least ten dozen with red chile pork. It was a big effort.

It started the day before, on December 23, when Mami would make the pork, simmering it for hours in a sauce made from local red chiles. We would have the pork with freshly made flour tortillas for dinner that night.

Then, early on the morning of Christmas Eve, Mami would go to the store to pick up the masa, a special corn-meal, for the tamales. Back home, she'd empty it into a large blue tub, where she would mix it with the other ingredients for the dough: salt, lard, and broth.

I was in charge of cleaning out the dry cornhusks that the tamales were wrapped in for cooking, making sure all the corn silk was removed before soaking the husks in water to soften them. After I finished, my mother would check my work and create a pile of rejects—cornhusks that hadn't been properly cleaned. It quickly became my goal to have zero rejects.

Once the cornhusks were thoroughly soaked and pliable, I would put them in a large bowl. My mom or aunt would spread a lump of dough inside a cornhusk and then spoon the meat filling into the middle of the flattened dough. They'd roll and fold the cornhusk into a neat rectangular bundle.

My mother would save some dough at the end, enough for a couple dozen dulce, or sweet, tamales. Instead of red chile pork, she would add sugar and pecans to the masa. All of the tamales would cook in large pots for an hour or two, filling the house with their savory smell.

After the tamales were done, Mami would switch to making buñuelos, a favorite pastry of Mario's. She would mix up the sweet flour dough and roll it out in circles. When I was in junior high school, to get the dough extra thin, my mother would use my basketball, which I would wash and she would cover with a thin dishtowel. Rolling the basketball on the towel, she'd stretch out the dough until it was almost translucent. Pulling carefully so as not to tear them, she would lay out the buñuelos on the counter, which she'd covered with paper, letting the pastries air-dry before frying them in hot oil. After spooning them out of the frying pan, my mother would dust the buñuelos with cinnamon and sugar.

By the time Mami had finished the buñuelos, the tamales would also be ready. I marveled at her efficiency, at the way everything happened like clockwork even though I never saw her write out plans or directions on paper. She counted out the tamales by dozens and shared them with whomever had helped make them. Every year, my mother would take tamales and other homemade goodies to Hermana Díaz and Hermana Cortéz, another friend from church. It was one of my tasks to deliver holiday treats to other friends, neighbors, and family members. I loved the warm reception I received as people told me over and over how much they loved my mother.

While all this was going on, Papá was reading or watching television. He kept to himself—not in an unfriendly way, but he didn't join the party in the kitchen.

On Christmas Eve, after a long day of cooking, we would have family and friends over for dinner. Some of the friends who'd helped out with the tamales would stay and their families would come, and the Barbas — Tía Alma, Uncle Sam, and my cousins Debbie, Cathy, Sammy, Jacob, and Ana — would come too. Everyone would be in a wonderful mood. After we ate, we'd run around the house and play games with our cousins and friends while the grownups sat and talked.

We didn't have alcohol at our family dinners. Instead, my mother made hot cider and Mexican hot chocolate for our Christmas Eve dinner. This was partly because my family was Baptist and partly because my mother forbade my father to bring alcohol into the house. In the past, he'd sometimes had a problem controlling his drinking. Now he and Uncle Sam might enjoy an occasional beer, but that was all Mami would allow.

A few weeks before Christmas, my mother would have gotten out the holiday decorations. She nudged my father and Mario to string up the multicolored lights outside along the roof. Then, on Christmas Eve, we would add sand and a small candle to dozens of brown paper bags to make luminarias. As the sun was setting, we would line the sidewalk by our house with them. Sometimes other neighbors would join in and line their own sidewalks with luminarias, though most of our neighbors just had holiday lights.

After dinner, our guests would leave, and we'd pile into the family car. We'd drive around Las Cruces to see the Christmas lights in other neighborhoods, especially those in La Mesilla, a village of adobe buildings on the border of Las Cruces. Though our neighborhood was pretty and we thought our street was beautiful, not all the houses were decorated. But everyone in La Mesilla put out holiday lights, and they lined their lawns and sidewalks with luminarias throughout the holiday season and especially on Christmas Eve.

In the neighborhoods with many luminarias, my father would turn off the headlights, driving slowly in the dark so we could see the rows and rows of flickering lights. In the back seat, we'd excitedly vie for window space, secure in the feeling that our family was together and happy. There would be Christmas carols on the radio, and we'd sing along, the only time I remember my family singing together. In the car, I could sing as loudly as I wanted, and everybody thought my voice was fine. By the time we got home, we were all tired, and we children were sent to bed right away.

On Christmas morning, we woke up to find stockings filled with hard candy, nuts, and an orange. When we would complain that it was just food, my mother would remind us that she had grown up in abject poverty, with no presents or stockings. She and her brothers and sisters were always hungry, so a stocking filled with food was a real gift. To my mother, the stocking was a sign that she could provide for her children. I knew that she filled them with love.

In the days leading up to Christmas, gifts would have accumulated in our living room. We would all have a few, but Mami always received more than anyone else. Many times when I was delivering Christmas food, a family member or a friend would hand me a wrapped present for my mother. The gifts were a reminder that she had a life outside of our family and that many people loved and admired her because she was always thinking of others. While we children looked forward to our own gifts, I was proud of Mami for receiving so many presents.

My parents had firm rules about not sneaking peeks or opening gifts before Christmas morning. They said that waiting was part of the magic of Christmas. We could touch the gifts and even rearrange them under the tree, but we weren't allowed to shake them. Still, we liked to count and organize the presents. We would sit by the tree and try to figure out what could be inside the boxes. When a gift didn't resemble anything that we might have asked for, we figured it was clothes, and we were usually right.

I was frequently the first one to open my eyes on Christmas morning. I'd wake Laura, then bang on the door of my brother's room before going into my parents' bedroom and shaking my mother's shoulder. Once we had all gathered around the tree, we could open the gifts.

My parents were good about getting us both practical gifts *and* presents that were fun. Mario was a fanatic for model airplanes. A model World War II airplane was always his first choice for a gift, and he assumed that was what the rest of us wanted as well. He would give models to our cousins Sammy and Jacob, then go to their house and build them. He received clothing, too, and so did Laura and I. These items were something special, like a more expensive jacket than we'd normally expect, not ordinary school clothes. Even our dog, Fito, always got a wrapped present, usually a rawhide chew. After all, he was a member of our family too!

By the end of Christmas Day, I'd be worn out by the preparations of the day before and the excitement of the day itself. Savoring the warm peace of the quiet house, I'd go to bed, filled with love for everyone in my family: my parents, Mario and Laura, our dog, my aunts and uncles and grandparents and cousins.

Mami liked to keep the house in order. With three—and later four—active children, she made sure that we always cleaned up after ourselves and made our beds. Even Laura had chores. Every December 26, I would wake to the sound of the vacuum cleaning up the needles from the Christmas tree. Before she made breakfast, my mother would take down the tree and put away all the ornaments. She disliked the sight of overflowing garbage cans, so later that morning, my father and Mario would haul the tree, still festooned with tinsel, and all the other trash to the dump. When they came back, we'd sit down to a lunch of leftovers. The outdoor Christmas lights could remain for another week, but inside, we had moved on. Now it was all about the new year.

Christmas in our house on Key Lane, 1968

CHAPTER 10

Learning to Save and Budget Through Cookies

B y the spring of third grade, I'd grown out of my Brownie uniform. The skirt was too short on me, and the blouse was too tight. The socks had worn out long ago, though I still liked to wear the headband sometimes.

I had real friends at school, Liz and Cindy and other Brownies in my troop who were also in my class. I sat with them at lunch and played with them at recess. We sometimes gave the two-fingered Brownie greeting when we saw one another at school. We had two stars on our too-small uniforms, one for each year we'd been Brownies.

We had done many things in those two years. We'd

made cornhusk dolls and tambourines out of paper plates. We'd played games like Sa Po Po, where we had to beat out rhythms in an order that went faster and faster until we all collapsed, laughing. We'd discovered the meaning of the Brownie name in a folktale about two little girls in faraway England who learned how to help around the house. We'd taken walks while singing the Brownie hiking song, which went, "We are the happy Brownies. We are the busy elves. We love to help each other, and of course we help ourselves." I loved being a busy Brownie elf!

Mami had made friends through Brownies too. She saw my troop leaders often and sometimes helped them with projects.

Although my Brownie uniform was too small, Mami wouldn't have to buy me a new one. Instead, at the end of the school year, I would join all the older Brownies in a ceremony. The troop leaders explained that we'd be "flying up" to Junior Girl Scouts, and next fall, we'd wear the green Junior uniform with a sash and a beret instead of the Brownie beanie. We'd all receive cloth Brownie wings to sew onto our new sashes. The wings meant that we'd belonged to a Brownie troop and we'd flown up. Then, as Juniors, we'd get to work earning badges, something we hadn't done as Brownies.

The Junior Girl Scouts had their first meeting in the school cafeteria on the very first Wednesday of fourth grade. I knew many of the new Juniors from our Brownie troop, but not all of them. There were some older girls there too, fifth and sixth graders. I thought they looked grown-up, full of confidence, their sashes already sprinkled with badges. Mrs. Davenport had flown up with our Junior troop, and we had a new troop leader, Mrs. Beeman, as well. We sat in a circle, and for the first time, I recited the Girl Scout Promise holding up three fingers instead of two, the way we had with the Brownie Promise.

After we'd gone around in a circle and introduced ourselves, Mrs. Beeman said she had a question.

"What would you like to do this year?" she asked us.

Girls spoke up excitedly. "I'd like to go on a bike trip," one girl said. Another said she wanted to go bird watching. Somebody else wanted to learn to cook. When one girl suggested camping, several others agreed.

Everyone seemed to think a camping trip would be fun. We voted and quickly decided that would be one of our activities. I would have said yes to anything. I was surprised that the troop leaders would let us decide for ourselves what we would be doing.

Since it would be our first overnight trip, we decided to go to a campsite that was part of Apodaca Park, right in Las Cruces. The leaders liked it because it was fenced in, and we could set up tents and build a fire to make s'mores. I didn't know what s'mores were, but the older girls cheered when someone mentioned them.

Before the meeting ended, Mrs. Beeman reminded us, "Don't forget to look through your handbooks this weekend. You can find ideas for badges to complete while we work on our camping trip and other activities."

Well, I didn't wait for the weekend. That very night, after finishing my homework, I thumbed through my Girl Scout guide, looking for descriptions of the badges. Juliette Low, the founder of the Girl Scouts, had said that badges were a symbol that we had learned something well enough to be prepared to give service in it. Each badge had a list of steps to be checked off to show mastery.

I liked the idea of badges such as Troop Camper, Outdoor Cook, and Cyclist, which our whole troop could accomplish together. I saw other badges that interested me too. I even made a list, picturing myself in my uniform with a sash full of colorful cloth badges for Health Aid, Musician, Books, and more. There was even a badge called Observer, which involved taking an adventure hike, looking for weather signs, and learning the constellations.

Still, for all my enthusiasm about badges and camping trips, I felt a knot settle slowly into my stomach. I loved the sound of the activities and the badges. But Mami had already bought my Junior uniform and a new handbook for Junior Girl Scouts. We didn't have extra money for trips and activities.

Maybe I couldn't be a Junior Scout after all, or maybe I could go to the meetings and earn a few simple badges, but nothing else.

At the next meeting, as we took our places in the circle, the other girls were buzzing with excitement, discussing their plans for the camping trip and the badges they wanted to earn. "Sylvia, is something wrong?" Mrs. Beeman asked.

Surprised to be singled out, I said that I didn't think my

family had the money for Junior Girl Scout activities. Then I looked down, ashamed.

Mrs. Beeman laughed. "Don't worry," she said. "We'll sell cookies!"

I looked around, confused. Was she laughing at me?

Then she elaborated: "Sylvia has a good point. The activities we've planned will cost money. But don't worry," she repeated. "We're going to earn the money to do the things we want to do. How are we going to do that?"

She looked around the room. "Cookies!" said one of the older Girl Scouts, echoing our troop leader.

Cookies? What did they mean? I saw some of the other new Juniors looking puzzled too.

The older girls explained that every year, girls across the country sold boxes of cookies—special cookies that you could buy only from the Girl Scouts—to raise money for their troop activities. Now it was our turn.

Mrs. Beeman's talk of earning money to fund our activities was new to me. I had my own savings account, the one I'd started so I could get a library card, and I'd been adding to it over the years. I liked the way the total in my passbook grew with each new deposit.

But my family lived paycheck to paycheck. Like all the mothers I knew except for Tía Alma, who was a schoolteacher, Mami didn't have a job, and Papá's salary barely paid for everything we needed. What's more, we were a family of six now. My baby brother, Armando, was born when I was eight, in January of my third-grade year. I was so excited; we hadn't had a new baby in the family since Laura was born.

My parents didn't have much money saved. We all loved Armando, a happy, active baby, but after he was born, my parents seemed even more worried about paying their bills. Mami was thrifty and good at finding ways to save money, but each new expense seemed to catch my parents by surprise. That was just how things were in my family.

Now the Girl Scouts were teaching me how to plan and save for the future. We talked about how much money we'd need for our activities, and Mrs. Beeman told us how much money we had in our bank account from the past year. I didn't know our troop already had a bank account!

We decided that we'd save the camping trip for the spring, when the weather turned mild. That would be many months from now and after the cookie sale, so we'd have the money for supplies. We talked about what would happen if it rained on the date we chose and how we would make alternative plans.

As we talked, I looked around at the other girls, amazed. In my family, we never discussed our future activities in this way, never made the connection between deciding what we wanted to do and planning in advance to be sure we had the money saved up. I loved my parents, but this was something new, something they couldn't teach me—and the Girl Scouts could.

Then we talked about badges. We were going to ride our bikes to the campground, meaning we could earn our Cyclist badge. We would learn the rules of traffic and some basic maintenance, like how to oil our chains and how to make sure the tires were pumped up for a smoother ride. We would be camping outdoors, so we could work on our Troop Camper badge: making charts for all of the camp jobs, and planning games and nature walks.

I raised my hand. "What about the Observer badge?" I asked. "That has hiking and learning about the outdoors." The other girls and my troop leaders liked that idea, and

Mrs. Davenport asked me to plan the activities we would have to do to earn the badge.

The previous year I had begged my parents for a bicycle, and Mario had begged them too on my behalf, because I rode his bike so often. At last I had been given my own bike, a green Western Flyer. Mami told me that three times around our block was a mile, and I'd spend whole afternoons riding around the block, counting the miles.

Now, with the rest of my troop, I started working on the Cyclist badge. I realized that all by myself, I could keep my bicycle in order and ride it safely, just by following the steps to earn a Girl Scout badge. After I learned to check the tire pressure, I checked it so often at the local gas station that the manager finally gave me my own personal air-pressure gauge. It even had a clip that I could fasten to my pocket. I liked the way the steps in the Cyclist badge progressed, from easy challenges like stopping and starting to larger projects for our whole troop, like planning an all-day expedition and a community safety activity. Not every badge needed to involve the whole troop, but I liked the ones that did.

Over the next few weeks, we continued to plan our camping expedition. We'd eat three meals on the trip—dinner, breakfast, and lunch—and we discussed what supplies we would need and how much they would cost. By the time we finished planning the camping trip, we had a budget.

Once we knew how much the trip would cost, Mrs. Beeman explained how the cookie sale worked. The camping trip would cost one hundred dollars, but it wasn't the only activity that we'd have to fund from cookie sales. We were planning a day of arts and crafts, and we needed to purchase art supplies. We needed materials to make new sit-upons. And later in the fall, we'd go on a hayride and have a barbecue.

Each box of cookies cost fifty cents and would earn our troop twenty-five cents. The other twenty-five cents paid for the cost of the cookies, and some of it also went to the local Girl Scout office. To earn the money for the camping trip, the hayride, and our other activities, the members of our troop would have to sell seventy-five boxes of cookies each.

Seventy-five boxes! Even with my extended family and our church, I couldn't sell that many cookies to people who knew me. I'd have to sell to neighbors and people I didn't know.

I had no idea how to begin.

But by now I wasn't surprised to learn that the Girl Scouts had a plan for how we would sell cookies.

Most important, whenever we were selling cookies, we had to wear our uniforms. The guide said, "The way you act when you wear your uniform shows that you really mean your Girl Scout Promise. You are proud of your uniform, so you keep it neat and clean." I'd have to keep my uniform in top shape at all times.

The first box of cookies I sold was to Mami. And she did not make it easy for me! I had never tasted a Girl Scout cookie, but I had a paper that showed pictures of the boxes and gave brief descriptions of the cookies. She said I had to tell her about all the different kinds of cookies before she would buy any of them.

I stood in front of her, wearing my uniform, straight and proud. "First," I said, "there are Chocolate Mints, chocolate cookies with a minty chocolate coating. Then there are

Peanut Butter Sandwiches, two crunchy peanut cookies with a creamy peanut butter filling between them." By now, my mouth was watering as I described buttery shortbread cookies, vanilla sandwich cookies, and the exotic Koko cookies, sugary circles topped with chocolate and flakes of coconut.

After I got through all five kinds of cookies, Mami didn't say anything at first. She looked thoughtful. I knew the cookies were an extravagance for us. When Papá went to visit his father, he frequently brought back cookies from Juárez, Mexico. One box cost less than these and contained dozens of cookies.

At last, Mami said, "I will buy a box of Peanut Butter Sandwich cookies."

I wasn't surprised at this. Mami loved peanut butter. Then she said, "Let's buy a box of Shortbreads and two of the Chocolate Mints."

Four boxes! Mami was as committed to the cookie sale as I was, I realized. I grinned at her, thrilled that I had made my first sale.

After I'd written it down on my order form, Mami told me I was allowed to sell cookies to other customers. Seventy-one boxes to go! I had a lot of work to do.

Even before she made me sell her that first box of cook-ies, Mami had been involved in Girl Scouts. It had begun back when I was in Brownies, when she started bringing treats to our meetings. As she became friendly with Mrs. Davenport and Mrs. Provine, she began helping them.

Until she had met my troop leaders, Mami didn't have friendships with anyone outside our immediate family who spoke English. My troop leaders were housewives, like her. Over time, they and Mami had gotten to know one another well, and my mother's English had improved by leaps and bounds.

One day while I was in Brownies, my leaders had asked Mami if she could help collect and keep track of our membership dues. She said yes, and she took her responsi-bilities very seriously. She helped our leaders keep our fi-nancial records in order, and I got used to seeing her with sleeves for coins and plastic pouches for dollar bills. As she gained experience, Mami's confidence increased.

When I flew up to Juniors, Mami flew up in another way—by becoming a United States citizen. She already had a green card that allowed her to be a legal resident. All four of us children, along with Papá, had been born in the United

States, so we were citizens. Now it was Mami's turn, as my troop leaders put her in touch with a service that helped her complete the process.

Papá hadn't seemed too interested when Mami first told us that she had decided to do this. He said he didn't see that it was necessary. "Why would you need to be a citizen when you have your green card?" he'd asked, mystified.

Ever since he'd been offered the job years earlier at the White Sands Missile Range, Papá had worked hard. He never missed a day, even if he was sick, and he was proud that he was able to support his family, as most fathers did in those days. As far as he was concerned, Mami needed only to keep house and care for his children, and now he said that if she got her citizenship, he wasn't sure she would need him for anything except his paycheck.

I had no idea what Papá meant, but around that time, he was often short-tempered. Mami said he had been passed over for a big promotion at work, and this had upset him.

Still, Papá could see how hard Mami was studying for the citizenship exam. She had to know all about American history and government, and she was determined not to miss a single question on the test. On the day she became a citizen of the United States, he told her he was very proud of her. We all were!

Now Mrs. Beeman showed how much trust she had in Mami by asking her to be in charge of the cookie sale. It was a big job, but Mami loved challenges and learning new things, so she said yes.

In our meetings, we had talked about the way to sell cookies. Our troop leaders had taught us how Girl Scouts were supposed to approach a sale. Once we had asked someone to buy our cookies, we weren't allowed to leave until they had placed an order or had told us no three times.

If someone said no the first time, I had to ask, "Why don't you want the cookies?" If they said they couldn't eat them, I could suggest they take them into work, school, or church. If they said they didn't like the flavors, I could point out a new flavor they might not have tried before. And if they said they didn't have any money, I could tell them that they didn't have to pay when they ordered the cookies, only when I delivered them. And it was convenient: I would bring those cookies right to their door!

After I sold my first boxes of cookies to Mami, I sold

more boxes to our relatives and members of our church. I still had a long way to go to meet my goal of selling seventy-five boxes, though. The next step was to start selling to people in our neighborhood.

While Mami kept tabs on how far along we were with our cookie sales, I was knocking on doors. Every day after school, except when we had our Girl Scout meeting, I'd change into my uniform. I'd make sure the blouse was tucked in and my sash was neat. Then I'd take my cookie order form and a pencil and set out. In those days, you could choose whether to sell cookies on your own or with a friend. Most of the time I went with another Girl Scout, a friend from my troop, but on the streets around our house, I went by myself.

The first time I knocked on the door of someone I didn't know, it was a neighbor whom I had seen but never spoken to. She came to the door in a pink bathrobe. I asked her if she wanted to buy some Girl Scout cookies. To my surprise, she said no.

I looked at her, my feet rooted to the spot, as I heard Mrs. Beeman's voice in my head, telling us never to leave a sale until a customer had told us no three times. "Is there someone else at home who might want to buy cookies?" I blurted out. Again the lady in the pink bathrobe said no.

Finally I asked, "Is there someone's day you want to make by giving them Girl Scout cookies?" At that, the woman smiled, and she finally said yes. As we discussed the various cookies, I was overjoyed, just the way I had felt with Mami.

Through sales like this one, I learned persistence. That gave me the confidence to talk to more strangers. The numbers started to add up: five, ten, twenty boxes. Soon I was keeping a list of streets in my neighborhood and doors I had knocked on.

At each door, I would start by introducing myself and saying the name of my Girl Scout troop. Then I would describe the different kinds of cookies. Sometimes the person would buy a box or two right away—they might have tried Girl Scout cookies before. One or two people even told me their daughters used to be Girl Scouts.

But some people wouldn't buy cookies, even when I asked them three times. They weren't rude, exactly, but they didn't let me spend much time talking to them. So I'd go on to another house, and another.

By the time I had sold seventy-five boxes, I knew how to make a sale. I was confident, when I rang each doorbell, that I could turn a potential customer's *no* into a *yes*. I'd earned the right to go on our camping trip, too, because I'd raised the money we needed for me to go. My seventy-five boxes had earned $18.75 for our troop!

Selling cookies completely changed the way I thought about my life. I had learned invaluable skills: how to sell, and how to create opportunity for my Girl Scout troop— and for me. I could create possibilities for myself. That gave me confidence and the courage to dream big dreams.

As the cookie sale drew to an end, Mami was in charge of collecting order forms from all the girls in my troop. She totaled up how many boxes of each cookie had been sold by each girl and sent in our troop's order to the regional Girl Scout headquarters. Mami came to our next troop meeting to tell us the total number of boxes we'd sold and how much we'd earned for our troop. We all cheered! It was a lot of money. I especially liked it when Mrs. Beeman told us we'd earned more than the troop had the past year or the year before.

Then we had to wait a few weeks for the cookies to be delivered to our troop leader's home. They arrived in big cartons marked with the names of the cookies inside: Chocolate Mints, Shortbread, Peanut Butter Sandwiches, and more. We each had to use our order forms to make a stack of the cookies we'd ordered, right in Mrs. Beeman's living room. The stacks were tall, too big for any of us to carry. Our leaders told us to leave the boxes where they were and see if anyone from our families could help us take our cookies home.

The simplest way to bring the cookies home would be in the car, I thought. Mami knew how to drive. That night, I asked her, and she agreed.

The next day was Saturday. I told Mami we could pick up the cookies any time that day. But Mami said we had to go to Mrs. Beeman's house early. She wouldn't let me take my cookies home until every other girl had picked up her boxes. Mami checked their counting too, just the way she'd overseen my stacks of coins long ago, when I broke open my cat bank. As each girl checked and double-checked her stacks of boxes, Mami nodded in approval, giving the girls permission to take their cookies away.

When the last girl left with her boxes, we took my own boxes home. Then I borrowed my brother's red wagon and delivered all the cookies I'd sold, except for the ones I would deliver in church the next day. After I'd carefully placed those in a stack, we had four boxes left, the ones Mami had bought from me on the first day of the cookie sale. She opened her purse and counted out two dollar bills, and I handed her the four boxes. She looked at them, as if considering which one to try first, then opened a box of Peanut Butter Sandwiches. She gave one cookie to Laura and one to me, and then she picked one for herself.

I took a bite, and peanut butter flavor flooded my mouth. Laura had already gobbled down her cookie. "Muy sabrosa," Mami said.

I smiled. I'd earned this cookie. "Delicious!" I replied.

CHAPTER 11

Our Family's Love of the Library

While Mami was making friends in our new neighborhood and volunteering with my Girl Scout troop, Papá was doing what he had always done. He visited his family, his mother and sister near us in Las Cruces and his own Papá in El Paso. He made sure Mario and I were doing well in school and hugged my little sister each night when he came home from work.

He got up at five thirty every weekday morning to go to work. Then, on Saturdays, he'd sleep late. Mami didn't like it when he did that, especially when she had chores for him to do.

Papá knew everything. He loved facts and knowledge,

and he loved to explain things, especially to his children. Mario and I spoke two languages, but Papá spoke three: Spanish, English, and German. He'd learned German in college and used it in his advanced chemistry courses, and he kept up his reading skills all his life.

Sometimes my father would goad Mario by pitting the two of us in a contest, usually over a history or a geography question. "Mario and Sylvia," he'd say, "let's see who can name the most state capitals." Even though my brother was older, occasionally I knew the right answer before he did.

When that happened, my father would chide my brother. "Beaten by a girl, Mario?" he'd say, and Mario would be angry. I'd feel a little sorry for him, but that didn't keep me from trying my hardest to beat him every single time.

Because he was a boy, Mario got the lion's share of Papá's attention. Even when I won a contest, Papá seemed to pay more attention to Mario's loss than to my win. Laura always knew how to get Papá to notice her with a hug and a kiss, but between Mario and my father's books, newspapers, and chemical journals, Papá didn't have much time for me.

Besides, no matter how hard I tried, I didn't win Papá's

competitions too often. Mario was really smart, and because he was two years older than I was, he had covered more subjects in school. He and my father both loved history, especially military history, and Mario liked to read about famous battles. Because they were so interested in World War II, I grew up knowing a lot about D-Day, the Battle of the Bulge, and other battles from that war.

Papá knew so much about history because he loved to read. Not a day passed when he didn't have his nose in a book, at least some of the time. Whenever a new bestselling thriller would come out in paperback, he'd buy a copy and spend the weekend devouring it. Back then, it seemed every store had racks filled with paperbacks—even the convenience store offered racks of books. Papá liked the library, too. Every other Sunday he would go to the university library, and on Saturdays, if he wasn't visiting his father in El Paso, he'd often go to our local library. If we wanted to spend time with him, that was where we went too. When we were younger, Papá would take Mario to the library, but I had to beg to go with him, and he'd be stern with me, telling me not to bother him once we were there. Now that we were older, though, he never minded us tagging along.

Both before and after we moved to Kay Lane, our public library was the Branigan branch in Las Cruces. It was an adobe building constructed during the 1930s and had a mural painted on the arch above the checkout counter. The mural showed a Spanish Catholic monk from the year 1610 presenting an open book to a group of Native Americans, including a little boy. *Would the monk have read the book to me?* I wondered. Did he ever read a story to that little boy?

We all liked to visit the library, but Mario went with Papá every chance he got. If Papá was doing something else on a Saturday, Mario would go on his own, and he would stay as long as he could, just reading in a corner. Sometimes Mami would call the library and say, "Send Mario home. It's time for supper."

The librarians were nice, and they got to know my family well, greeting us by name whenever we visited. We knew their names too. But they had rules. One was that we had to be quiet. Another was that up until age twelve, children were allowed to take out books only from the children's section.

Whenever we arrived at the library, Papá would go right away to the display of newspapers and magazines. "Be good," he would tell us, pulling the day's newspaper off a rack as we headed into the children's room. If we wanted to find him, we'd look for him in the adult reading room. He never came with us or helped us choose our books, and we didn't expect him to.

I decided that if I wasn't allowed beyond the children's room, I would simply read everything on its shelves. Maybe then the librarians would let me read books from the rest of the library.

Without the library, I would never have read as much as I did. We had very few books at home, and I read each one cover to cover until I had nearly memorized it. One time, when I was just learning to read, we were in El Paso and stopped in a department store with a bookstore. My parents bought a book for me about a nurse named Clara Barton. It was the first time I'd ever read about a woman who did important things, even helping to win a war. On the way home that day, I sat on my mother's lap and read, not even noticing when we turned into our driveway in Las Cruces.

My mother hadn't yet learned to read English, so when

I came to a word I didn't know, she would spell it out in Spanish to my father. He would then pronounce the word in English. I read that book so many times, Mami learned the whole story in English. I loved reading about someone who had lived so long ago and was still remembered now, a century after her work as a nurse in the civil war.

Once I had my library card, I discovered a whole series of biographies about the childhoods of famous people, and those books became my favorites. I liked knowing that famous people like Abraham Lincoln, Florence Nightingale, and Harriet Tubman had been kids like me, wondering what they would do when they grew up.

We could take out a couple of books from the library each week, and over time I really did read all the books in the children's room.

I had loved to read ever since my days in Head Start. When I was in first grade, my mother learned about books that were sold with records. Children could follow along in the book as they listened to somebody read the story on the record. Since Mami couldn't read to me in English, she bought me a portable record player that folded up like a suitcase so I could listen to the recorded books, and when she could afford them, she bought me those books, too.

I understood that this was Mami's way of encouraging me to learn, and it made me feel special. I used the record player for reading, but I also let Laura listen to music with it. When she was a little older, she'd play the record of "Waltzing Matilda," her favorite song, over and over and over. I got tired of the song, but I never tired of my sister's joy in it.

There were some books that we couldn't check out of the library, such as the large, heavy encyclopedias. Sometimes I'd just flip through the *D* volume, reading about Denmark, dodoes, drums, and anything else that caught my eye. Then I'd switch to *B* and learn about Belgium, beetles, and basketball.

After Mario and I started school, my parents bought us the *World Book Encyclopedia,* a set of twenty illustrated books. Each letter of the alphabet had its own volume, with the exception of some of the less common letters, which shared volumes. My parents also bought a world atlas. These reference books were a big investment, and Mario and I devoured them. We loved the anatomy section of the encyclopedia, where translucent pages revealed the human body's skeletal, digestive, and respiratory systems and even its layers of skin.

In those days, there were no computers in school or in our homes. If we wanted to find out something, the library was our Internet and the librarians were our Google. We could ask them any question, and they would help us find the answer. That was how we learned about the world outside of Las Cruces.

One day, a friend of mine from Girl Scouts said a bowling league, just for kids, was forming at the local bowling alley. If we joined, we'd be on a team, playing against kids from other teams in the league.

No one in my family had ever been bowling before. I wasn't even really sure what bowling was, but I liked the idea of being on a team. And because of my Girl Scout experience, I knew I could learn how to bowl if I took it step by step, just like when I earned a badge. So the next time I went to the library, I asked the librarian, "Do you have any books about bowling?"

"Just a minute," she said. She disappeared into the nonfiction section for adults and came back a minute later with a small book. Even though it wasn't from the children's room, she said I could take it home. The cover showed a smiling teenager holding a ball that was bigger than his head. Excited, I checked out the book.

That weekend, I read the book from cover to cover. I learned all the rules by heart and pored over the drawings that showed how to pick up the ball and fling it down the alley. If you knocked over all ten pins at once, that was a strike, which was the best way to score. But if you left any pins standing and knocked them over on your next try, the bowling rules said that was a spare. You got two turns to knock down ten pins, and those two turns were called a frame. I didn't know why they used those words, but I liked knowing the terms because it meant I was learning something new.

After I studied the drawings, I practiced in my bedroom, gripping an imaginary ball and sending it down the alley with a flourish. I kept the door closed so no one would see me looking in the mirror to be sure I was standing just like the person in the pictures. Finally, on Saturday, my friend and I walked over to the bowling alley and signed up for a team. I had saved my weekly allowance so I could pay the fees and rent bowling shoes.

I quickly found out that real bowling wasn't exactly the same as pretend bowling in my bedroom. But by the time my library book was due, I could knock down most of the pins, and so could the other kids on my team. Before long, we were winning trophies, and I was one of the team's best bowlers.

If it hadn't been for the badges I'd earned in Girl Scouts, I would never have had the courage to learn how to bowl. Because of the badges, I knew that I could teach myself to fulfill a goal and work as a member of a team. With a little help from the library, I used those skills to join the bowling league. I still remember the smooth texture of my first bowling trophy against my fingers as I gripped it tightly, filled with excitement, running home to show my mother.

Since Papá was a chemist, he needed to keep up with chemical journals, so twice a month, he'd go to the library at New Mexico State University, in Las Cruces. Over time, Papá had become more and more preoccupied with his job, and he continued to work very hard. Sometimes he and Mami would argue about things we kids didn't understand. When we argued that way, we'd sometimes get a spanking if Papá was home and lost his temper because we were too loud. If he wasn't around, Mami would lock the two of us who were arguing in the bathroom until we were friends again. But when Papá and Mami disagreed, there was nobody who could tell them to behave.

After Papá and Mami argued, my father would spend more time at the library. When Mario and I went with him to the Branigan branch, I'd always leave after a couple of hours. I loved to read, but I couldn't sit inside all day. I had to run around! But Mario was like Papá, his nose always in a book, spending all day in the library.

Still, I did my fair share of reading. By the time I was in fourth grade, I was reading everything I could get my hands on. I was at the top of my class. Then something happened that changed the way I thought about my future.

I knew that I would be going to college one day, though most of the adult women I knew had finished their education in high school—or even grade school, as Mami had.

Except for my teachers, Tía Alma was the only woman I knew with a college degree. When I thought of college, I pictured a school like Alameda Elementary, except that I would be older and taller. I might even have my own car!

I didn't understand yet that in college, students focused on one course of study, and that unlike our public schools, colleges cost money to attend. I just knew I wanted to go.

I didn't talk about these thoughts with anyone at the time, though. I was more interested in earning Girl Scout badges, riding my bike, playing games, and reading every book in the library. I enjoyed my bowling team and I loved basketball, my favorite game at recess. High school and even junior high seemed very far away.

My fourth-grade teacher's son had gone away to college, and he had sent her photographs of different universities around the world. One day, my teacher decided to share them with us. She set up a slide projector with all of the photographs, showing large modern brick complexes and buildings whose dark stone walls were covered with ivy. Then one slide jumped out at me.

This college didn't look like any place I knew in Las Cruces. The buildings were beautiful, with red tile roofs and rounded archways. And the surrounding lawns were the greenest I had ever seen.

I raised my hand. "What's that one?" I asked.

"That's Stanford University, in California," said my teacher.

"I want to go there," I said.

She walked over to my desk. "It's a really great school," she said, smiling. "You're a smart girl. If you want to go there, you can."

A college was a real place, I realized. It wasn't just something people talked about to get kids to do their homework. I could pick a college and go there, even if it was far away from Las Cruces, New Mexico. If the other girls I knew wanted to get married and have children, I could still choose to do other things. I could be someone who had adventures, like the girls in the Disney shows.

I was nine years old, living in a small desert town. And on that day I decided I would go to Stanford.

Me in fifth grade — get ready world!

CHAPTER 12

A Troop for Everyone

One of the best things about Junior Girl Scouts was earning badges. We had earned some on our first camping trip together, like Cyclist and Troop Camper. The trip had been only one overnight, but I'd loved every minute as we set up our tents in Apodaca Park, prepared our meals, and sang songs around the campfire while we roasted marshmallows for s'mores. Even going to sleep outdoors, surrounded by my friends in their own sleeping bags, was exciting.

The first year of Juniors, when I was in fourth grade, I did the Observer badge. I loved the weekends spent outdoors, looking for cloud formations, constellations, and insects going about their business. I even gave a presentation to my troop about the rock formations in the nearby Organ Mountains. Each time I earned a new badge, I would proudly sew it onto my sash.

After our camping trip, Mrs. Beeman said to me, "You know, Sylvia, I remember you looking at the stars."

She had noticed how much I loved to look up and wonder at the stars, drinking in the majesty of countless points of light as they stretched into the black velvet of infinity. Sometimes after sunset I would climb the mulberry tree in our front yard and stare at the heavens. I had read that Robert Goddard—the father of modern rocketry—also used to climb a tree, gaze at the stars, and dream about visiting outer space.

"Is there a badge for you somewhere in the stars?" my troop leader asked now. "Maybe studying space?"

After this conversation, I checked my *Junior Girl Scout Handbook,* but I didn't see any badge that fit. Then, several months later, in my second year of Juniors, Mrs. Beeman brought up the subject again, telling me that the handbook for Cadette Girl Scouts, who were older, had a Science badge. She thought I might enjoy the projects since I'd liked the Observer badge so much.

I wasn't so sure I wanted to earn the Science badge. The other girls in my troop were about to start working on their Cooking badge, and I wanted to do that, too. Mrs. Beeman encouraged me, though, saying I could earn both a Cooking and a Science badge, and she lent me the *Cadette Girl Scout Handbook* so I could see what the requirements were.

After the meeting, I read about the Science badge. It sounded like fun, so I decided to try it. I took a package of tomato seeds and sprouted them by keeping them in moist newspapers. Then I planted the seeds outside, and soon I was able to pick tomatoes for us to eat. I added chemicals to growing plants to see what would happen. For another requirement, I had to collect newspaper clippings about the space program and atomic energy. And I had to learn about levers and demonstrate how they worked.

I enjoyed fulfilling the requirements for the Science badge. But the handbook said that to complete the badge, I also had to design a science project of my own. At first, I didn't know what that could be. Then I had an idea: maybe I could do a project with Estes rockets.

In those days, everybody talked about space travel. When I was four years old, President Kennedy had vowed to put a man on the moon, and now, with President Johnson promising the same thing, NASA—the National Aeronautics and Space Administration—was working to make it happen. So lots of kids—and their parents and teachers—were excited by rockets, and by astronauts too, such as John Glenn, the first American to orbit the earth.

Estes rockets were model rockets that could actually be launched high into the air. I'd heard about them from my brother and cousins, and sometimes I heard boys at school talking about them. If they could shoot model rockets into the sky, why couldn't I?

Mario built models all the time, so I asked him, "Where can I get Estes rockets?" He said the store where he bought his plastic World War II airplane models—Hobby Hut—might carry them. But he also received catalogs in the mail, and he had an Estes model rocket catalog in his bedroom.

We looked at the catalog together, and Mario helped me figure out the differences between the various rockets, how hard they might be to put together, and how much they cost. I picked out a model, took money from my savings account, and sent in my order. After three long weeks, my rocket arrived in the mail.

The rocket kit contained a cardboard tube, fins and a nose cone cut from balsa wood, a plastic parachute, string cords, and instructions. The rocket engines came in a separate package of three. They were self-contained, with solid fuel propellant. Mario helped me glue the fins into place and showed me where the nose cone would go. Then we put the parachute together, and finally, we painted the rocket. Everything had to be assembled precisely for the rocket to fly true and for the parachute recovery system to work. Waiting for the glue and paint to dry seemed to take forever. I was eager to launch my rocket.

Since the engines were started by electric igniters, Mario had to borrow a battery-operated launcher from a friend. On launch day, Mario and I carried the launcher and rocket to a nearby empty lot. We folded the parachute just so and slid it into the front of the rocket's body; then we clamped the nose cone into place. We inserted one of the engines into the tail of the rocket, crimped an igniter into the engine nozzle, and connected the igniter to the launcher's wires.

With the rocket mounted on the launcher's guide rod, we stepped back and I recited an official-sounding NASA countdown, starting with "Ten." At "Liftoff!" I twisted the launch key to ignite the engine.

Nothing happened. The rocket sat on the launcher.

After some trial and error, we learned that the electric igniters were finicky. If the rocket didn't launch, we had to wait a couple of minutes to make sure the engine hadn't started to burn before adjusting the igniter. After several tries, at last I turned the key and the little rocket zoomed upward in a trail of smoke.

Several hundred feet above us, the engine detonated the ejection charge with a pop. We watched as the parachute unfurled, and the rocket floated toward the ground. I'd done it! We ran after the rocket since we weren't sure where it would land. I was thrilled to find it nearby, undamaged and ready for another flight. That afternoon we launched it two more times.

And soon I had earned my Science badge.

While I had been firing off rockets, most of the other girls in my troop had begun working on the Cooking badge. I helped Mami in the kitchen sometimes, but aside from our Christmas celebrations, I'd never been too interested in cooking. Still, at our meetings, the rest of the girls were excited about the recipes they'd been trying. I didn't want to miss out on anything.

Since most of the girls had already started earning the badge, I needed to hurry if I wanted to catch up. The first requirement was that I know how to measure out dry, liquid, and solid ingredients. To demonstrate that, our troop leaders decided we would have to cook something from a recipe. We would do that at home and tell our troop about our experience. I liked cookies, so I decided to make peanut butter cookies.

Even though Mami had been learning English, all of our cookbooks were in Spanish. I could read some Spanish, but not as well as I could read in English. "Do you need help?" Mami asked me.

"No, I know what to do," I answered confidently. After all, I'd been helping Mami and Tía Angélica with their baking since I was little. While Tía Angélica didn't live with us these days, she was a talented cook, and I loved being in the kitchen with her. Now I found a cookie recipe, and even though it was in Spanish, I thought I could figure out the directions.

Feeling grown-up, I pulled out a mixing bowl and added the ingredients—sugar, butter, an egg—carefully checking each one before mixing it with the rest. I added flour, using the cup measure, then coaxed peanut butter into and out of the measuring cup with a spatula. I saw that the recipe called for baking powder and baking soda, one half teaspoon each. I read the measurements in the Spanish cookbook and translated them into English in my head.

I was almost done with measuring! The next ingredient was salt. Moving quickly now, I read the quantity in Spanish, thinking that the *c* in "cucharadita" meant cup. A cup of salt sounded like a lot, but that was what the recipe called for. I measured out a cup of salt from the container and dumped it into the bowl.

Once all the ingredients were mixed in, I pinched off small pieces of the cookie dough and rolled them into balls. I lined up the balls neatly on the cookie sheet and flattened each one with a fork, making a crisscross pattern. I set the timer and watched to be sure they didn't get too brown. They smelled wonderful, and they looked perfect.

The first batch of cookies was cooling on the racks, and I was getting ready to slide a second batch into the oven when Mario wandered into the kitchen. Without even asking, he grabbed a cookie and stuffed it into his mouth. Then he rushed to the sink and spat it out. "This is awful!" he exclaimed.

I thought he was teasing me! Indignantly, I started to answer back, and Mami came into the kitchen to see what the fuss was about. When Mario told her the cookie tasted horrible, she took one from the rack. After a very small bite, she looked at me. "Sylvia, explain to me how you mixed up the cookie dough. Go through every step."

Step by step, we went over the recipe, in English and

in Spanish. When I explained that I thought "1 cucharadita" meant one cup of salt, Mami's eyes widened.

"You added a cup of salt to the cookies!" She was aghast. "'Cucharadita' is this!" she said, waving the teaspoon in front of my face. "'Taza' is the word for cup, like here." She pointed to the measurement for flour in the recipe. "There are few recipes that would ever require a cup of salt!" Even before she finished speaking, I knew she was right. I had measured out all the other ingredients correctly, translating the Spanish words for cup and teaspoon—taza and cucharadita—into English, but I wasn't careful at the end of the recipe, and I had made a mistake in translating the measurement for salt.

I could see Mario smirking, and even Mami had to hide a smile. I felt like crying. I knew the mistake was all my fault.

I cleaned up the kitchen, wrapping the cookies and the rest of the dough in newspaper so I wouldn't have to see them in the garbage bin. All the other girls were getting their Cooking badges, and now I'd be the only Scout in my troop without that badge on my sash.

I asked Mami if I could try again.

Now Mami looked sad. "Peanut butter is expensive," she said. "We can't afford more."

She went into the pantry, and I followed her. "What do we have?" she asked, sounding thoughtful. We had flour, tomato sauce, and yeast. "Let's make some pizza," she said.

I found a recipe right on the package of yeast. As I got out the ingredients, Mami asked if I needed help. The directions were in English this time, so I said no. I could read all the words in the recipe without any trouble!

I opened the package of yeast and poured it into a mixing bowl. The directions said to add warm water. Remembering how important it was to get the temperature right for the rocket to launch, I heated a pan of water on the stove. When it boiled, I measured out a cup and poured it over the yeast. I mixed in the flour, salt, and cooking oil and kneaded the dough for a long time, until it was a smooth ball. I put it back in the bowl with a towel over the top and waited for the dough to rise.

At first, I checked the pizza dough every few minutes, until Mami came into the kitchen and suggested I go outside and play. When I came back an hour later, the dough was exactly the same size. Nothing had changed, except the top had dried out.

Once again, Mami went through the recipe with me, asking what I'd done at each step. Then she said, "Sylvia, we have another packet of yeast. Throw this out and let's try again."

She explained that I had killed the yeast with the boiling water. I hadn't really understood that yeast is alive and that it creates the bubbles that make the dough rise. The water had been too hot, just as it would have been too hot if I'd spilled it on myself.

This time Mami didn't ask me; she stayed around. When we got to the part about pouring warm water onto the yeast, she told me to test the temperature by sprinkling a drop or two onto my wrist. If the water burned my skin, it was too hot. It had to be just a bit uncomfortable.

I added the water to the yeast, gave it a quick stir, and waited ten minutes. The mixture was brownish-gray, with bubbles rising to the surface, just like a chemical reaction. It didn't look like something I would want to eat. Still, I added flour, salt, oil, and more warm water, mixed it with a wooden spoon, and then kneaded it on a wooden board. The dough felt warm to my touch, and this time it rose when I left it in the bowl for an hour. I rolled it out, spread tomato sauce and cheese on top, and baked it in the oven. Even Mario said the pizza tasted good.

I remembered that as I had kneaded the dough, I had thought that this process was just like building and launching my Estes rocket. In both science and cooking, you had to follow the directions, and you had to get the heat just right. Making a science experiment work was like cooking: if something didn't work, you could figure out why and try again. And if I could cook, I could do science!

When my Cooking badge finally arrived, I sewed it with pride onto my sash, right next to the Science badge.

By the time I got the Cooking badge, in the fall of sixth grade, I wasn't the only member of my family who had joined a Girl Scout troop. Mami had been in charge of my troop's cookie sale for two years, and she'd seen how the Girl Scouts had changed my life. They had changed her life too. *Why couldn't Laura be a Girl Scout?* she wondered.

We all knew Laura was different from everyone else in our family, and she knew it too. She probably didn't remember her life before she got meningitis, but she knew that she had trouble learning. She often got frustrated when she saw other children learning the alphabet or doing things that were hard for her. She loved to draw, but she had difficulty with motor skills, such as inserting a straw through the top of a drinking cup. Not long after she enrolled in Alameda Elementary School, the teachers called Mami in for a meeting: Laura couldn't keep up with the other first graders.

The teachers suggested that Mami enroll Laura in a school for children with learning disabilities on the other side of Las Cruces. Laura soon came to love her new school, and, now in second grade, she was even learning the alphabet. We all tried to be sure nobody made fun of her, but sometimes it happened anyway. Still, Laura was always good-tempered and loving.

Mami decided it was time for Laura to enroll in Brownies, just like I had. She formed a small troop of girls from Laura's special-needs school, with Mami as their leader. I would come to their meetings and help when I had time.

All the girls in Laura's troop were in her class at school. Some of them, like Martha and Tina, were her good friends.

Some of the girls had Down syndrome or other developmental disabilities.

Mami had to make sure the girls in Laura's troop had more time than the girls in my troop had to complete their activities and craft projects, and many of the girls needed extra help. Maybe they didn't do as much as we had when I was in Brownies, but they did go on a trip to the park that first year, and they wove sit-upons, the way my troop had.

Best of all, when Laura put on her Brownie uniform, and later, when she was a Junior and then a Cadette, she was a regular kid. She was a Girl Scout, as I was before her, and just like all the other Girl Scouts we knew. Even Papá could see how happy that made her.

One time, years later, after Laura had crossed the bridge into Cadettes, Mami did something for Laura's troop that even got into the newspaper. Every year on various holidays, a Girl Scout troop would post the colors—raise the United States flag—at the local adobe courthouse. Why couldn't Laura's troop do this? Mami asked herself.

My mother lobbied for Laura's troop to post the colors. The people at the courthouse were skeptical. The girls in Laura's troop were from the "other" school. They sometimes behaved oddly. Children and occasionally even adults who didn't know any better made fun of them.

But Mami insisted that Laura's troop could do it. She trained them like a drill sergeant.

Tina was selected to carry the American flag, which really upset my sister. She wanted the honor of posting the flag, but my mother did not play favorites. Laura did lead the audience in the Pledge of Allegiance, her hand proudly over her heart.

The day they posted the colors, the girls in my sister's troop were beautifully turned out, with pressed, immaculate uniforms. They marched in perfect unison with the flag held high. At the courthouse, they presented the colors and everyone cheered. It was one of the proudest days of Laura's life—and of Mami's.

That day, when I saw my sister and her friends doing such a normal thing, being good citizens, I cried tears of joy. They weren't the special kids that day, the ones who couldn't learn in the same way or keep up with everyone else. Instead, they were just ordinary Girl Scouts performing their civic duty. I have never forgotten that.

Over time, the Girl Scouts were good for all three of

us: Mami, Laura, and me. We each conquered new skills, gained confidence, and learned how to be more involved in the world around us. Because Mami needed to know about bank accounts to run the cookie sale, my troop leaders helped her learn about the banking system. As she grew more self-confident, Mami even opened her own savings account. In those days, women needed their husbands' permission to open a bank account, and many married women didn't have their own separate accounts. Papá was annoyed, but in the end he gave his permission. At the end of my time in Junior Girl Scouts, I loved the way my sash looked, with its rows of colorful badges. I was proud of what the badges represented, each one showing that I'd mastered a new skill. Every badge reminded me of the community to which I belonged. I could look at the badges and remember the conversations I'd had with my troop leaders and with other girls about skills we were learning. Whether those skills belonged to the kitchen or to the outdoors, we were all gaining confidence in our own abilities.

Laura in her Girl Scout uniform, 1972

CHAPTER 13

Planning for Survival

When I was young, I could never understand how my mother calculated time. At school, the day was divided into blocks of minutes. At 9:30, I knew we'd put down our books to stand and stretch at our desks. At 12:15, we'd have lunch, and afterward, recess at 12:45. I liked stacking my books when the bell rang and lining up at the front of the room at the same time each day.

But at home, time moved differently. "We're going to the store," Mami would say. As soon as she said that, a neighbor would drop by, and Mami would offer her a cup of coffee and a slice of cake. They'd start chatting about somebody's niece who was getting married, and an hour later, nobody had gone to the store. Then Armando, the baby, would wake up hungry, and we'd be out of milk, and Mami would just laugh and send Mario or me to the Piggly Wiggly.

In my parents' culture, people were a priority. So Mami would always choose visiting with a neighbor or relative over running an errand or getting somewhere on time. To treat people any other way would be rude.

Sometimes this confused me. I could never tell what would happen next. We would go to Chihuahua, in Mexico, to visit Mami's family. But when we got there, Mami didn't seem to be in any rush. "We'll meet up with them later," she'd say.

"Where?" I always wanted to know.

Mami would just shake her head. "You'll see," she'd say. Then she'd repeat, "We'll meet up with them," leaving me puzzled.

Later in the day, we'd be shopping downtown or enjoying a fruit drink in a café, and sure enough, a couple of our aunts and cousins would come around the corner. Everyone's face would light up, and they'd rush over to us. It was like magic, I thought while being enveloped in warm hugs.

But I was still mystified about how Mami had known this would happen.

My friends from Anglo families never had this experience. Their families always planned when and where to meet. I loved the way Mami welcomed people into our lives without seeming to plan in advance. I could see how much she valued our friends and relations and how much they loved her for that. I knew it must be part of my culture. But I was beginning to realize how my family's world was different from that of my classmates. I didn't know why that was. It just was.

On our yearly summer trips to see Mami's mother in Chihuahua, Mexico, or on Papá's trips to El Paso every other week to see his papá, Papá drove a series of used cars. We'd own one for a while, maybe a year or two, and then it would break down, so Papá would sell it and buy another from a neighbor or a relative.

By the time I was nine, Papá had gotten fed up with cars that broke down. "They're lemons," he said. "All of them."

I knew "lemon" means a machine that doesn't work

well, but I didn't see the connection to the fruit. Was a broken car sour? Full of juice? I sometimes heard gasoline referred to as juice, even though gas was poisonous.

Soon after Papá's comment, he and Mami bought a new car, a two-door Pontiac LeMans. It was a big, beautiful coupe, painted aqua — the color of the ocean — with an enormous, graceful chrome bumper. The car had bucket seats up front, a roomy back seat, and a powerful V-8 engine. It wasn't the most practical family car, but my parents were very proud of it. I was proud of it too. And I was happy to see Mami and Papá working together to get such a nice car for us.

At first, our new car had plenty of pep, but over time, the engine would sometimes stutter and it wouldn't speed up when we got on the highway. Papá would pump the gas pedal or shift the gear, and after a few seconds, the car would surge ahead. It didn't occur to him to have the car serviced, or even to change the oil. When one of our cars stopped working, it was a mysterious process. All we knew was that it occurred too frequently, and at the most inconvenient times.

By the summer of 1968, when I turned eleven, we'd had

the LeMans for a couple of years. The seats were a little stained, and there were some dings in the paint, but it still looked sporty, like a car on television, and not like our other jalopies.

When school started that August, everyone in my sixth-grade class was talking about the Olympics. They would be starting the next month in Mexico City.

Mami and Papá were filled with pride that the Olympics were in Mexico, and they decided that our family should attend. One day, when I came home from school, Mami told me we'd be leaving the next morning. We would be out of school for two weeks, and I would miss two Girl Scout meetings! But I knew how important this trip was to my parents, who ordinarily would never let us skip school unless we were very sick.

Mexico City was one thousand two hundred miles away—even farther away from Las Cruces than South Dakota! We would start with a long drive through the Chihuahuan Desert to visit my grandmother and some of Mami's sisters in Chihuahua. Then we'd continue on to Mexico City.

Much as we had for our previous trips to Mexico, we packed the night before leaving. The next day was Saturday, and Mami woke us up before sunrise. We dressed in our good clothes, since we'd be visiting family first. Mario, Laura, and I climbed into the back seat, and Papá got behind the wheel—he always drove on our family trips. Even after she got her license, Mami never drove when Papá was in the car. She sat up front holding Armando. Back then, most babies and small children didn't sit in car seats. Our car had seat belts, but we didn't use them.

That morning, my mother had packed a breakfast so we could eat on the way. She never let us eat in the car, so we made a quick stop to eat our breakfast.

In the back seat, Mario, Laura, and I usually bickered over who had to sit in the middle. Mario and I played games to see how many different license plates we could spot, and Laura liked to look for children in the back seats of the cars we passed. We were used to the forty-five-minute drive to El Paso and familiar with the six-hour ride to Chihuahua, but I wondered what the long journey to Mexico City would be like.

Mami and Papá were proud to be attending the Olympics in the country where their families were from, but they hadn't planned ahead. Neither of them had thought to order tickets, arrange for hotels, or prepare the car for a round trip of nearly two thousand five hundred miles, much of it through the desert.

Still, we were excited as we crossed into Mexico and received the TURISTA sticker on the windshield, branding us tourists in the country where Mami was born. Driving away from Juárez, the border city, we ventured onto the road that would take us into the desert.

We'd pass a few very small towns on the way to Chihuahua, but most of our trip would take us through open desert. My mother had packed a little water and a few snacks, which we ate in Juárez. Mami planned to stop in some of the towns to buy cheese and other local provisions.

Soon we had passed the last buildings on the outskirts of Juárez. The landscape became largely flat, broken up by gullies and small hills. We saw shrubs and cacti but few other signs of life. We settled back in our seats, Armando dozing in Mami's arms up front, Laura chattering about a bird circling overhead. An hour passed, and I felt sleepy.

Suddenly, we heard a loud squeal from the engine. Red lights flashed on the instrument panel, and Papá quickly pulled over to the side of the road. Something was very wrong. We all piled out of the car, and my father opened the hood. Peering into the workings of the motor, we all saw the torn fan belt. I didn't know much about engines, but I knew this wasn't good.

As my parents talked about what to do, we stood huddled by the car. It was a scorching desert day, and few cars or trucks were on the road.

I knew Papá couldn't fix the car. And nobody in those days would have expected a woman like Mami to understand how a car's engine worked. Besides, we didn't have a spare fan belt or tools.

After a while, Mario and I grew bored and went to play in the sand dunes. Mami wasn't happy about our doing so, since we were dressed in our good clothes, but she soon relented, since there was nothing else for us to do.

Aside from the cacti and other plants, the desert looked empty of life. But as I sank to my knees, running my hands through the hot sand, I saw a scorpion, its tail curved over its back. We spied a smooth path in the sand, so we knew we'd better stay on the lookout for snakes, too.

After a while, we grew hungry and thirsty, but we

didn't complain. There was water for Armando in his bottle, but there was nothing for anyone else to drink, since we'd planned to buy drinks en route. And there was nothing we could do about that. I wiped the sweat off my brow, thinking about our Girl Scout trips, which we always planned ahead. We always brought along enough food and water too.

At home, my mother assumed that my father would manage the exterior of the house, the lawns, and the car, just as Uncle Sam did in Tía Alma's family. Unfortunately, that didn't happen: Papá wasn't interested in home maintenance. In his free time he watched the news on television or read or talked with my brother or uncle about politics. But he just wasn't a handy guy.

Papá still took for granted that he was in charge of our family. But that day in the desert, he couldn't fix the car. He didn't have a solution to the problem we faced, and we all knew it would get worse if we stayed where we were.

We had only one option. Stranded in the desert, hungry and thirsty, we started walking along the road to Chihuahua, over the hot asphalt. I wondered how we would ever get out of this jam. This was not the first time one of our cars had broken down, although it had never happened this far from home. I knew it didn't have to be this way.

Even though we hadn't gone too far, we were all hot and tired when a bus finally appeared on the highway. My parents waved frantically, and it stopped.

My mother and father decided that Papá would have to go back to the car and wait for someone to come along and help. Mami herded the four of us kids into the bus, and other passengers moved over and made space for us to sit. Taking pity, some of them offered us drinks and food.

Luckily, the bus was going all the way to Chihuahua. We made it to my grandmother's house that night, and the next day, my father joined us. He said the highway patrol had stopped and fixed the car.

The following morning, Papá drove the LeMans to a mechanic in my grandmother's town and had it inspected. The new fan belt was working fine. We'd been lucky: the engine wasn't damaged. We were off to Mexico City and the Olympics!

After a day of driving with no mishaps, we spent the night in a magnificent old hotel in Zacatecas. Back on the road, as we approached Mexico City, we saw bright colors and flowers everywhere. We learned later that the government had provided paint and flowers so people could spruce up their homes and streets and the country could put on its best face for the world's attention.

Mami and Papá had said we would be staying in a hotel, but as they discussed where to go, it became clear that neither of them had made a reservation. Mami thought it was Papá's job, and Papá hadn't thought it was necessary. Now we learned that every hotel in the city was fully booked for the Olympics. Where would we stay?

We tried a few hotels in downtown Mexico City, and people looked at Papá as if he were crazy even for asking if a room was available. Then he got lucky. At the desk of the next hotel he tried, a clerk said that a customer with a reservation had been delayed. We could have his room, as long as we understood that when he arrived, we would have to leave.

Everything was going to work out, I thought. Before that trip, I had stayed in a hotel only once before, in Phoenix, Arizona, and I couldn't wait to see our room. In the lobby, while we waited for Papá to finish checking us in, a man with very dark skin was staring at my family. He asked me a question, and I couldn't believe that he was speaking with a British accent. I thought all British people were fair-skinned. The man said he was from Bermuda, an island in the Atlantic Ocean near North Carolina. He told me that he was staring because he was surprised that a brown-skinned family like mine was speaking English and not Spanish. He gave me an enameled pin that Bermuda had manufactured just for the Olympics.

After we registered and left our suitcases in our room, we walked outside. There was so much to see! In the park near our hotel, there were Olympics displays and people selling all kinds of goods—and there were swans swimming in a pond. The weather was beautiful, and my whole family was happy to have reached our destination.

It turned out, though, that to attend the Olympics, we needed to buy tickets. That hadn't occurred to my parents before we left on our trip, and by now, tickets to the popular matches and games were sold out. At last, Papá was able to purchase tickets to a sport we'd never heard of—water polo. We watched teams of men from Greece and Yugoslavia in an enormous swimming pool, competing to score points by throwing a ball into a goal.

It was all very exciting, but we spent only two nights in our hotel. Although we weren't able to buy more Olympics tickets, we visited Xochimilco, with its famous floating gardens, and the National Museum of Anthropology. When we returned to the hotel for a third night, we were told that the customer who had originally reserved our room had shown up. We would have to leave.

The hotel staff must have felt sorry for us, because they called around and found us a room outside the city, in a facility run by nuns. We spent that night in a bedroom attic. Even though our hostesses welcomed us politely, I felt awkward as we climbed the stairs.

The next morning, over coffee, my parents discussed what to do. It would be a long drive back to Mexico City if we wanted to see more of the Olympics, and there was no guarantee that even if Papá tried again, we'd be able to get more tickets. I could tell that Mami was angry and frustrated with Papá for not planning ahead. But I also knew that making plans just wasn't in Papá's nature. And Mami knew it too.

In the end, instead of returning to the Olympics, we drove west along forested mountain roads, spent one night in Guadalajara, and then drove all the way back across the desert to Las Cruces. This time, the car behaved.

When I returned to school after two weeks away, my classmates couldn't believe where I'd gone. Even though I'd seen very little of the actual Olympics, they were impressed.

We'd had a good time on our trip, even if my parents hadn't planned it well. Things could have been a lot worse. It wasn't until we were home that I remembered something that had happened two years earlier, when another lack of planning had almost led to disaster.

One cold winter morning when I was about nine, I awoke to find my mother shaking me, jerking my arm, shouting, "Wake up!" with a note of desperation in her voice. I looked at Mami, confused. My head hurt, and I wanted to go back to sleep. The sun was brighter than it usually was when Mami got us up for school. Armando was crying in Mami's arms, and Fito was barking. Laura was holding Mami's skirt, looking worried.

Mami didn't let me go back to sleep. I couldn't seem to walk by myself, so she dragged me outside and made me lie down on the cool dew-covered grass. Laura sat down next to me, and I saw that Mario was already outside, also lying in the grass.

I felt dizzy, and my stomach hurt. My head pounded and I was shivering, and all I wanted was to go back to sleep.

Mami went back inside, still holding Armando, and a minute later, I saw that all the windows had been opened, even though it was the middle of winter.

Papá was at work, and he had taken our car that day because my mother had not felt well. Mami told us that instead of waking us up after Papá left, she had fallen back asleep. She had woken up, groggy, to find Fito licking her face and barking. Her stomach hurt, and then she threw up, right on the floor. She knew something was very wrong, and that was when she woke us up.

Whatever the problem was, Mami wasn't going to let me or Mario miss school. She wouldn't let us go back into the house at first, but she went inside by herself to turn off the furnace. She got our clothes and made us get dressed on the screened-in porch. Then she brought us back inside for a quick breakfast, although my stomach still hurt and I didn't want to eat. Shaking and crying, Mami called Papá at work to tell him what had happened. Afterward, calmer, she walked us to school.

My head felt clearer after the walk, but I still felt sick and drowsy. I sat at my desk but found I couldn't pay attention, and my teacher asked what was wrong. When I looked down instead of answering, her expression changed to one of concern. "Sylvia, don't you feel well?" she asked.

I shook my head. The teacher gave me a look but left me alone. I stayed in school all day, and after a while I felt a little better.

When we got home, a man had come to fix the furnace. "When was the last time you changed the furnace filter?" he asked.

My mother shook her head. She had no idea.

The man explained that if you did not change the filter regularly, a gas called carbon monoxide built up inside the house. This poisonous gas can be deadly if too much of it is inhaled. That's what had made me—and the whole family—feel so sick all day. If Fito hadn't made Mami wake up, we all could have died.

By the next day, we felt fine, and I didn't think about the episode for a long time.

But after we returned from Mexico, with the memory of the car breakdown fresh in my mind, I remember thinking that we didn't have to live this way. And I thought about our broken furnace two years earlier. Now I understood why some adults, such as the men who fixed our furnace or our car, had looked at my parents with pity for not knowing what to do. They knew that to live your life without getting sick or breaking down in the desert, you had to make plans and maintain your property, your house, and your car.

Over and over in Girl Scouts, I had learned that planning ahead and doing things properly could help you get what you wanted. We sometimes talked about college in our troop meetings, and I knew that college cost money—a lot of money. Mami had helped me start a bank account, but she never reminded me to add to it. All on my own, I was using my bank account to save, because I knew I'd need to pay for college myself.

Now I realized that I might have to be the one who did the planning ahead for my family, to make sure we never again got stranded in the desert or became sick because of a dirty furnace filter. Just as I had when I sold Girl Scout cookies to create the opportunity for adventures, I could plan ahead to keep my family safe. But I was still in sixth grade at Alameda Elementary School. It would take me some time to learn how to do this.

When I was little, Papá sometimes lost his temper and spanked one of us kids for misbehaving. I never thought I deserved it at the time, of course, but I knew better than to argue back when he got angry. The only child who never got a spanking was Laura. Papá was always gentle with her, even when she did something he didn't like.

A couple of times at night, when they were arguing, I had heard Papá hit Mami. When that happened, Mario and I would stand in the hall, listening and sobbing, not knowing what to do. One time, overwhelmed with despair and shame, we walked miles across town to Uncle Sam's house. Tía Alma took us in and put us to bed, and the next day, Mami came to take us home. Nothing was ever said to us about the matter. In those days, domestic violence was considered private family business, and outsiders seldom intervened.

After we returned from Mexico City, Papá was working very long hours. He said he needed to make up the time he'd taken off to take us all on vacation. He and Mami often quarreled—about the trip, about chores she wanted him to do, and most of all, about money.

I didn't think too much about it, though. I was excited to be nearly finished with elementary school. When sixth grade ended, I'd graduate and go on to junior high school—in my town, that's what we called the school we attended for seventh, eighth, and ninth grades. Not only that, but just as I'd "flown up" from Brownies to Juniors, now I would "cross the bridge" from Juniors to Cadettes. I thought the older girls in the Cadette handbook looked grown-up and glamorous.

In sixth grade, my bowling team met every Saturday morning. One day, I came home from bowling practice to find Mami crying. Her hair was untidy, and she was pacing back and forth in the kitchen.

Mami told me that she and Papá had had a terrible fight, and he had hit her the way he had in the past. She said she was leaving my father and taking us with her. We were going to move to California, where Tía Angélica was living at the time.

I realized then that Papá must have gone out, but that

wasn't unusual for a Saturday. Mario wasn't home either. Mami asked me to help her get ready to leave. We had to pack right away, she insisted. It was too much.

I couldn't take in what she was telling me. Instead of helping her, I ran out of the house and into the street.

Seeing a group of neighborhood kids who were playing kickball, I ran up to them and asked to join the game. But before I could take my place, Mami came out and pulled me aside. Still crying, her voice shaking, she pleaded with me to help her.

I couldn't do it. I loved my mother, but I was over-whelmed. I knew Papá had a temper, and the fight must have been horrible. I had never seen Mami so distraught.

Mario's bike was lying on our front lawn. I grabbed it by the handlebars and jumped onto its seat, and I took off with my mother calling after me.

I rode to the school, circling in and out of the parking lot and playground. Then I headed downtown. I hadn't had lunch, but I wasn't hungry. I didn't know how long I stayed on the bike—I didn't even notice where I was, passing streets and parks and churches.

Finally, without being aware of what I was doing, I

parked the bike by the door of the library. In the children's room, I picked up books I had already read, flipping through the pages, not taking in the words. I was still in shock.

I didn't know how much time had passed when I heard my name and saw the librarian standing in front of me. "The library is closing, Sylvia," she said gently. "You need to go home now."

When she asked if I wanted to check out any books, I shook my head. I didn't have the energy to speak. I found Mario's bike where I had left it outside. It was late afternoon, I realized, and cooler now that the sun was setting.

I rode slowly home, taking my time on the neighborhood streets before turning onto Kay Lane. The car was in the driveway, so I knew Papá was home. The lights in the house glowed a familiar warm yellow.

I pushed the bike through the side gate into the backyard. I could see through the patio doors that my father was inside, and no one seemed to be arguing or fighting. I went around to the front door and slipped quietly inside and down the hall to my room.

In an instant, Mami followed me and closed the door behind her. She said she had told Papá that if he ever hit her again, she would leave him and take all of us kids with her. Her voice was calm, but tears ran down her cheeks. She apologized to me and asked me to forgive her.

I hated to see her so upset. "Don't cry," I told her.

Mami wiped her eyes and her voice became deadly serious. I recognized her tone from years earlier, when she told Papá she was getting her driver's license.

"If he ever hits me again, I'm leaving," she repeated. Then, sounding more ordinary, she asked if I was hungry.

I shook my head. I didn't want to leave my room, didn't want to see Papá or Mario or Laura or even Armando. I wanted Mami to go away, and as if reading my mind, she left quietly. After a while, Laura came in with her doll, wanting me to play with her, but I ignored her, pretending to be asleep.

I was numb, and I just wanted the day to end. But it would be a long time before I felt comfortable around Papá or even Mami. I still had to obey them, but I felt that by fighting, my parents were acting like children. Not only that, but my family was going in separate directions, and I wasn't at all sure where I belonged.

Mario, Laura, Mami, Armando, and me

CHAPTER 14

Changes at School
and at Home

After my parents' fight, things seemed easier on the surface, though we were all struggling underneath. Papá was still working hard, and he would bring home fat manila folders from his office. In the evenings, instead of turning on the television or burying himself in a book, he'd come into my bedroom and spread his papers out on my desk. If he tried to do that on our dining room table, Mami would make him clear them off in time for supper. But the summer after sixth grade, I didn't use my desk for homework, so he could leave his papers there.

From listening to the grownups, I gradually learned that Papá was getting ready to take the United States government to court. He had been passed over for promotion at the White Sands Missile Range, where he had worked since I was little, and had been exposed to dangerous chemicals without the proper protection. He had become convinced that these things had happened in part because of his Mexican heritage. Now he was preparing for the lawsuit. He might not have filed the lawsuit on his own, but Uncle Sam, who also worked at the missile range, encouraged Papá. In spite of their differences, Mami supported Papá too.

Papá's lawsuit would take a long time, though. Meanwhile, something happened that summer that was exciting for everyone, adults and children alike.

One evening in July, Papá, Mami, Mario, Laura, little Armando, and I sat in front of our new color television, watching as, far away, an astronaut climbed down a ladder from a tiny space capsule onto the surface of the moon.

"That's one small step for a man," said Neil Armstrong, the first human ever to step onto the moon, "one giant leap for mankind."

And womankind, too, I thought. I pictured myself one day working with astronauts and rockets. Maybe I'd be one of those people at NASA headquarters counting down the spaceship launch, just like I had with my Estes rocket.

Not long after the moon landing, in August of 1969, I started seventh grade at Alameda Junior High School. I would stay there for three years, before beginning high school in tenth grade.

Earlier that spring, I had crossed the bridge from Junior Girl Scouts to Cadettes. But once I started junior high school, I was surprised to find myself less involved with the Girl Scouts. We didn't have a troop leader to help us plan activities, and I was spending more time on schoolwork. I had new interests, like band and basketball. I had new friends as well.

Most of my new friends were in the school band. I'd started playing the drums, and every day before school, we'd meet outside the band room. Cynthia played French horn. Lyn played the clarinet and guitar, and she loved to sing. Terry also played the clarinet, and Vicki played the saxophone.

I loved having a group of friends to hang out with, even if I didn't see them much after school. Most of them lived in another neighborhood, too far to visit very often on a bicycle during the school year. I had a couple of other friends, Charmagne and Kathy, who were in honors classes with us, but they weren't in band. I also had neighborhood friends, Phyllis and Cindy.

I didn't think much about the fact that almost all of these girls were Anglo. One of them had a Mexican grandparent, but their families weren't Mexican in origin, like mine. Most of them were in honors classes with me, and they pushed me to do my best.

Terry and Cynthia lived on the same street. Terry's parents were divorced, and her father took care of her and her brother. Cynthia was one of five siblings. She was Mormon and often was busy with her church. She and I were both very competitive and liked sports and any situation where we could compete. Lyn lived in another subdivision. She was one of three kids, and her parents were always pushing her and her siblings to do well in school. Vicki didn't like school as much as we did, but she was fun, and her family had a horse. Her parents were older and they taught her how to drive when she was in junior high, before she was eligible for a driver's license. When we went to her house, three or four of us would cram into their small Opel GT, and Vicki would drive around. She and I talked on the phone more than our other friends, although in some ways I was closer to Cynthia and Lyn. Sometimes I missed being a Girl Scout, but I loved having a large group of friends.

While I wasn't part of a Girl Scout troop, I helped out with Laura's troop sometimes and I still treasured the confidence I'd gained from my years in the Girl Scouts. Not long after I started in my new school, though, that confidence got me into trouble.

In junior high, all girls were expected to take a class called home economics, where they were taught to cook and sew. When I saw it on my schedule, I refused to go.

I was not the sort of student who normally disobeyed my teachers. Even I was a little surprised at my defiance. I didn't mind cooking; after all, I had earned the Girl Scout Cooking badge with my homemade pizza. And while I didn't like sewing as much as Mami did, she had taught me the basics, and it wasn't hard. I didn't know why I didn't want to go to home economics. I just didn't! Thinking about the class made my stomach hurt. And so when the bell rang on the first day of school and all the girls headed down the hall to home economics while all the boys went to shop class—where they would learn to use tools—I just stayed in my seat and pulled out a book.

"Sylvia?" I looked up to see my teacher standing in front of me. "Aren't you supposed to be in class?"

"I'm not going," I said. Inside, I was shaking a little, but I met my teacher's eyes and kept my voice steady. I was scared, but I wasn't backing down, and my teacher could see that.

It was unusual that a student would refuse to go to class, especially a good student like me. Two years earlier, when Mario was in seventh grade, it was a rule that all the boys took shop class and all the girls took home economics. Back then, I might have been forced to go, but now it was 1969, and times were changing. More women were going to college. Like Mami, some women were opening their own bank accounts. Some were getting jobs outside the home, in offices and places where only men had worked in the past. Some schools had stopped requiring home economics and shop classes. But at that time, at our school, only boys could take shop and only girls could take home economics.

The day after my first refusal, my teacher persuaded me to give the class a try. The home economics teacher was a thin lady who explained in a crisp tone that we would sew aprons, then finish them off with a colorful rickrack trim. She was giving all the girls detailed instructions, and I could see that she knew her subject well.

My friends in class were happy to see me, but I did not want to make that apron! To me it represented a future of cooking for my family instead of working at a job, and I hated that idea, though I didn't completely know why.

After school that day, I went to see the principal and told him I wanted to drop the class. He tried to talk me out of it, but in the end, he gave me a piece of paper that he called a waiver. If Papá signed it, he said, I wouldn't have to take home economics.

That night, I told Mami and Papá that I didn't want to take the class. Mami didn't mind: she had already taught me much of what I would have learned in home economics.

But Papá refused to sign the waiver. Even if I already knew how to cook and sew, he said, I was a girl, and this class was where I belonged.

A few years earlier, I wouldn't have challenged Papá.

Although I might not have agreed with him, I would have accepted that he knew best. But now, I refused to go every day to a class that was preparing me to be a homemaker. I was going to college, and I needed to learn other things besides cooking and sewing. And that's what I told Papá.

Mami agreed with me, and she convinced Papá that I was right. He was not happy to have both of us arguing against him, but eventually he signed the paper anyway. In the end, I thought he might have just been tired of arguing. Whatever the reason, I had permission to skip the class.

In the place of home economics, I was assigned to an extra math class. My friends couldn't believe I'd prefer to learn more math, especially algebra, than attend a class where we learned to sew and cook. They were smart girls, but they didn't mind the break from honors classes. I was happier with my new math class, though, and never regretted what I'd done.

A few years later, when I was in college, boys and girls at my junior high had the choice of shop class or home economics, and my brother Armando took home economics.

He liked to sew, and he had my mother's skill with crafts. He really enjoyed the class.

The conversation with my parents about home economics came during a troubled time with my father.

Following my parents' big fight the year before, I had lost all respect for my father for a time. I was so angry with him that I stopped calling him "sir."

Papá had never forgotten his time in the United States Army, and he liked it when we children responded, "Yes, sir," when he spoke to us. Fathers in our traditional culture could be strict, and Papá was, but in the past, I had also seen that he loved us. Now I could not respect him, and that set us up for an epic battle of wills. When Papá was pushed, he lost his temper, except with Laura, whom he always treated gently. By not saying "sir," I was pushing him.

For a while, I would even eat at the kitchen counter rather than at the dining room table with Papá. For Sunday dinners, when we all ate as a family, I sat apart, because I no longer wanted to afford him that respect. He tried to get me to sit at the family table, especially when his mother was eating Sunday dinner with us, but I refused, and my mother told him to leave me alone. I would sometimes join in when Papá and Mario were discussing politics or the military — or the moon launch — but most of the time, I avoided having anything to do with my father.

This tension came to a head once when I was in seventh grade, and Armando, who was a busy, active four-year-old, did something that annoyed my father. We all knew when Papá was about to lose his temper, and sure enough, he lifted his hand, about to strike. Armando cowered, tears starting down his face even before the spanking, and I rushed forward to stand between my father and my little brother. I stood, tense and waiting, expecting Papá to hit me instead of Armando.

And then, to my surprise, Mario joined me, gently pushing Armando back as he faced Papá beside me. We all stood frozen in place.

What happened next was something I could not have predicted: Papá backed down. Turning, not meeting our gazes, he left the room. Nobody followed him, and a minute later, I went to my bedroom. I didn't want to talk to anyone, not even Mami.

After that, my father never hit Armando again. And I learned that as competitive as Mario and I could be with each other, there were times when my older brother could be an ally.

And I needed Mario, because Papá and I would get on each other's nerves. We clashed frequently, as I continued to ignore his advice and commands and sassed him back whenever I could. I often retreated to my room, realizing Mami couldn't help me too much with my father, and I would lie on my bed and concentrate on my homework. I had discovered that after one of those arguments, running through math problems in my head would calm me, so I could get to sleep. But life felt more unsettled in junior high school, and that wasn't changing any time soon.

Me and Armando, 1970

CHAPTER 15

Hoops, Hotheads, Courts, and Cars

I liked school for a lot of reasons, but if I had to pick the one thing I looked forward to most, it would be playing basketball. I had always loved running around, and basketball was a sport that let me do just that.

In elementary school, as soon as we were dismissed from the cafeteria to the playground for recess, I would run to the padlocked box that held the sports equipment. When the recess teacher opened it, I would grab a basketball before the boys took them all, then rush out to the two black T-shaped asphalt courts.

I would run up and down beside the boys, practicing

dribbling, trying to grab their ball on the rebound, shooting lay-ups. I was one of the few girls who would play alongside them, and I quickly discovered that the boys expected me to shoot "granny style," tossing the ball underhand. I would never do that!

When I was playing basketball, I didn't care how hot and sweaty I got or that my hair slipped loose from my braids and my socks were falling down.

Sometimes after recess, my teacher would send me to the girls' room to wash my face and clean up. She never told the boys to do this, no matter how sweaty they were. I didn't care. If we had outdoor recess that day, I was going to play basketball.

On weekends, I would ride my bike by the school, hoping to see one of my classmates playing basketball so I could join in.

The only time I skipped basketball at recess was when the Girl Scouts had a meeting after school. I didn't want my uniform to be untidy. On those days, I'd spend recess with girls from my troop, talking or sometimes jumping rope or playing hopscotch.

· · ·

Mami was the gift buyer in our family, and she always tried to give us the Christmas presents we wanted, as long as she and Papá could afford them. The year I was in sixth grade, I wanted a basketball with a backboard and rim more than anything. In the lead-up to the holiday, I saw more gifts appearing under the tree, but nothing in the shape of a basketball or a rim and backboard.

I wasn't worried, though. My parents often held back the bigger gifts until the night of Christmas Eve, since Laura and Armando still believed in Santa Claus. I felt sure I knew what would be waiting for me under the tree when the day arrived.

Early Christmas morning, my siblings and I ran to the tree. There were Hot Wheels for Armando, clothes and dolls for Laura, and models for Mario, but for me, there were only flat, rectangular boxes.

I slowly opened the biggest box and found a green winter ski jacket. Under other circumstances, I would have loved it.

I couldn't keep my disappointment from Mami. Our family of six lived modestly, and I knew that my next chance for a basketball was when my birthday came in August.

I liked the jacket, I really did, but August was eight long months away.

Sure enough, I did get a basketball on my next birthday, right before I started junior high. At my dinner place that night was a wrapped square box that could only be a ball. I tore it open and looked around, but that was my only present. Mami knew how much I wanted a basketball, but she hadn't understood that a basketball without a backboard and net was incomplete.

I was a little disappointed, but I knew money was tight. So I just put those items on my list for Christmas. In the meantime, I rode my bike to the school playground on weekends, steering with one hand and holding the ball under my other arm, hugging it close to my body. Now that I was in junior high, we didn't have recess. Girls played basketball in physical education class, but we had modified rules that allowed us to run and dribble only a few steps with the ball. That made the sport less exciting to me.

Still, I loved my basketball. I took good care of it, wiping it down each time I used it and even washing it with soap occasionally to keep it looking new. I counted down the months, weeks, and then days to Christmas.

Finally, Christmas arrived, and this time there was a basketball hoop under the tree. But once again, it wasn't quite what I had expected. I had my hoop, with its rim and net, but that was all. Nobody had thought to buy a backboard.

That day, I bugged my father to install the hoop on the roof of the carport. But Papá wasn't good with tools, and the rim was crooked. The shots that didn't go through the rim went wild: onto the carport or into the backyard. It didn't take too long before I realized I really had to have a backboard.

This time, I wasn't waiting until my next birthday in August. Instead, I headed for the library, where I looked up the dimensions of a regulation-size backboard. Then I took money from my savings account and went to a local hardware store.

I'd been to the hardware store before but never on my own, and I didn't think the clerk was used to seeing girls coming in by themselves. Still, he listened seriously when I explained what I wanted. I handed him the paper on which I'd copied the exact dimensions of the backboard, and he cut a piece of plywood to the right size. I paid for it and bought white paint and a brush. When I got home, I covered the plywood with paint. To outline a rectangle on the backboard above the rim, I asked Mario for some of the black paint he used for his models.

Mario gave me his paint, but when it was time to install the backboard, he said he was too busy to help me. Luckily, he had friends who came over and helped put up the basket at the right height on the carport. When that was done, I finally had my basketball court.

Now I could spend hours and hours in our driveway, practicing shots, dribbling, and playing endless games of Horse. Once, Mami came outside and had me show her how to dribble, but she couldn't master bouncing the ball the proper way. Papá never touched the basketball, and even Mario wasn't interested. So I practiced my skills on my own.

The lay-up was the best shot you could do in the driveway. On Sunday afternoons, I made a rule for myself that I wouldn't go inside until I had completed one hundred lay-ups. I tried to finish in time to see *Mutual of Omaha's Wild Kingdom* and *The Wonderful World of Disney*. In those days, television shows were broadcast at a specific time, usually just once, so if I missed a show, I had lost my one chance to see it. Even so, I was strict with myself, and I really worked on those lay-ups!

In our town, there were no girls' basketball teams. Sometimes I participated in daylong "play days," tournaments where girls got to play on teams against other girls. We used a modified set of rules, just the way we did in gym class. But the limitations didn't matter much to me. I still loved playing basketball. Every weekend for years, I would play with the neighborhood boys, who used the "regular" rules, though we often argued about what those rules actually were. Through practice I became really good at lay-ups, and it didn't bother me too much that I didn't have a team or that I might never have a way to show off my skills. That was just part of being a girl, I thought.

While I was spending long hours on the basketball court, Papá was in the final stages of suing the United States government, spending hours poring over his papers to prepare for his time in court. This was very stressful for him, and it made our battles all the more difficult. I tried to stay at a distance from Papá, but that wasn't always possible.

Then one night Papá and I clashed in a way we'd never done before. Until now, I had done well in all of my classes, but in eighth grade, my honors English grade slipped. My other grades were fine, but I didn't like my English teacher and I didn't like the class at all. Unfortunately, I wasn't successful in keeping my feelings to myself.

My teacher noted my attitude on my report card. Mami, not Papá, usually talked to our teachers when there was a problem, but now my father called the school and asked to speak to my English teacher.

At dinner that night, he asked me what was going on with my English class.

"Nothing much," I said.

Papá was not happy with that answer, and he told me I had to improve my grade, starting now.

"Yes," I answered, not sounding as if I meant it.

"Yes, sir," he reminded me.

If I'd been younger, before the fight with Armando one year earlier, I would have said, "Yes, sir," and ended the discussion. But I'd been angry at Papá for a long time, and he was easily irritated with me. "Yes," I repeated.

"Yes, sir!" Papá shouted, and he reached out and smacked my face.

I stood up and ran down the hall. Papá ran after me, and when he caught up, I hit him without thinking, just trying to protect myself. Then I dashed into my bedroom and slammed the door. Papá pushed it ajar, and Laura, who had followed us, darted into the room, crying. I pressed against the door with all my might, struggling to close it.

My father finally shoved the door open and stormed into the room, his eyes filled with rage, a look on his face I will never forget. He pulled off his belt and struck me once, twice. I curled up on the bed, and he kept hitting me, over and over, as Laura sobbed and begged him to stop.

Finally Mami came in and pulled Papá's arm down, and he stopped hitting me with the belt. "You wouldn't even beat an animal like that," she said.

When everyone else had left, Mario came into the room. He looked at me lying curled up on the bed. "Why don't you just say 'yes, sir'? You could make it easy on you and the rest of us."

Instead of answering, I crawled under the sheets and

closed my eyes, hearing him leave the room. I started reciting the multiplication tables in my head, wondering how high I could go.

Suddenly, I noticed an interesting pattern in the numbers. The product of five multiplied by any number was half the second number with a decimal point shifted to the right. Five times eight was forty, and half of eight was four. Shift the decimal point and add a zero, and you get forty. No matter what number I used, the result was the same.

By the time Laura came to bed, I was lost in the numbers, calm and focused. I'd forgotten about Papá—almost. I kept my eyes closed, not wanting to talk to Laura or Mami, but I kept doing number tricks in my head until I fell asleep.

The next day, I left the house early. Papá had already gone to work, and I wanted to avoid the others, even Mami. In school, I found my algebra teacher, Mr. Agnew, and shared my discovery. He showed me a couple of other math tricks, but I still liked the simplicity of the number five. Just as when I first learned to count in English, I found that I was happy and absorbed when I was concentrating on numbers. After a hard day, doing math problems in my head was soothing.

I still didn't have any easy answers to getting along with Papá, but I made sure to treat my English teacher with respect, and my grades in that subject slowly improved. Mostly, I just avoided my father, concentrating on my schoolwork, my friends, and band. And later that spring, Papá won his lawsuit against the United States government. A judge ruled that the managers at White Sands had not provided appropriate safety material, endangering his health. He was given a check for a lot of back pay.

My parents didn't have savings. Papá and Mami used the money from the lawsuit to build a new den—complete with a fireplace—in the rear of our house. They put the sewing machine in the room and the television, too. With six people and a dog in our small home, the new den gave us a bit more breathing space.

And Papá was happy when he won. The day the judge decided in his favor, my father took us all out for dinner at the A&W restaurant and then drove us around town. He was especially polite and considerate. Little by little, I breathed easier around him. And I remembered a promise I'd made.

After our trip to Mexico City in sixth grade, I'd promised myself I would use my Girl Scout experiences to help my family plan for the future and keep our house and possessions safe. With tensions easing at home, I finally had time to think. And I decided I needed to figure out what to do about this promise. The Girl Scout motto is "Be prepared," and that was what I planned to do.

I sensed that Papá and Mami would never save much money. They would never do basic car or home maintenance. I was saving money for myself, but I saw that my friends' parents had routines that my own parents lacked. Now that I was in junior high, I was embarrassed when our car broke down because our family hadn't planned ahead. The trouble was that I was still a kid. I didn't know where to begin.

One day toward the end of eighth grade, I saw a newspaper advertisement about a free class on car maintenance for women. Well, I wasn't a woman yet, but after our breakdown in the desert, I needed to learn about cars! I rode my bike to the address in the newspaper, which turned out to be a local car dealership, a shop that sold new and used cars. Inside, a handful of women were sitting on folding chairs.

The class was run by the man who owned the dealership. "Where's your mom?" he asked me. "Is she coming later?"

"No," I said, shaking my head. "It's just me."

He looked surprised. "Do you drive?" was his next question.

Well, of course I didn't drive! I was only thirteen. I shook my head again and told him I still wanted to learn about car maintenance.

He nodded, perhaps thinking I was a farm kid. There were many farms outside Las Cruces, and it wasn't unusual for kids from those families to drive at a young age while they helped with chores. Then he warned me to be careful and not get hurt. He waved at an empty chair, indicating I should sit down with the older women. "Now," he said, beginning the class. "We're here to teach you ladies how to get your hands dirty and keep your engines running smoothly."

I wasn't so sure I was a lady, but I listened carefully as

he described the basic mechanics of a combustion engine and how it ran. After that, we put on coveralls and took turns changing air filters and spark plugs in a car. Before we left, he promised us that next week, we would learn how to change the oil.

I was surprised that the older women were so enthusiastic. I expected them to complain about having to wear the ugly coveralls and get dirty. One or two of them made a face, but then someone said, "Knowing how to do this will save us so much money. If my husband won't do it, then I will!" All the other women nodded, and I grinned.

Leaving the class, I felt the way I had when I'd learned how to pass the scissors at my very first Brownie meeting. There was a proper way to take care of cars, and I could learn to do it, even if I wasn't old enough to drive. Even if Mami thought the maintenance of cars was men's work, that didn't have to be the case. Just ask my grown-up classmates at the car dealership!

On another evening, our instructor brought out a collection of handbooks. "These are car maintenance manuals," he said. We all flipped through them as he pointed out the diagrams that showed where everything was inside the engine and the directions that told how to keep the car in good shape.

"Where can I get one?" I asked him.

"Check your car's glove box," he said. "Most people keep them there."

I sped home on my green Western Flyer bicycle, propelled by my newly acquired knowledge. Jumping off my bike on the front lawn, I pulled open the passenger door of our Pontiac, popping open the glove box, where the thick owner's manual sat, unopened and unread. Inside was the maintenance schedule, just where the instructor had said it would be.

"Cars don't have to break down," he'd told us. "Keep them on a schedule of regular maintenance, and they'll run well for a long time."

I took the manual up to my bedroom, and I read it straight through.

From that moment until I left for college, I put our car on a maintenance schedule. Every few months, I'd change the oil. I bought car stands with my own money and would raise the car with a jack and drop it in place on the stands. I would unscrew the oil drain plug with a wrench and empty the oil into a plastic bucket. While the reservoir was emptying, I checked the air filter and the water levels in the radiator. Replacing the oil drain plug, I made sure I had it nice and snug—I didn't want any oil drips or leaks! Once I started doing this, we never again were stranded by a broken fan belt or anything else.

It was just as the Girl Scouts had taught me: be prepared, and you can take control of your life. Cars and furnaces don't have to break down, and people don't have to be stranded in the desert.

CHAPTER 16

Beating the Drums into High School

I don't know why I chose the drums. Everyone knew I loved the loud, brassy, bouncy music of Herb Alpert and the Tijuana Brass, so when I had the chance to join the school band in seventh grade, my family thought I'd pick up the trumpet. But something about the percussion instruments just fit. Although I didn't have a drum set at home, I practiced as much as I could at school. And when I was home, I'd pull out my drumsticks and beat a rhythm on any handy surface.

To play the drums well, you have to count, and by now, this was something I excelled at. By counting and keeping time in my head, I could provide a beat for the whole band. I loved that feeling.

I played drums in band all through junior high school, and in ninth grade I entered a statewide music competition for high school students. I was allowed to enter since ninth grade was considered high school in some school districts, even though it was still junior high for us. I practiced a timpani solo, "Carmen Miranda," with a piano accompanist, and when it was time for my audition, I played with a flourish and didn't make any mistakes at all.

A day or two later, the principal called me into his office. He told me that I had won the competition for best musical percussion soloist, and he announced it to the whole school over the loudspeaker. I was the first junior high student ever to win this statewide high school competition.

My parents didn't seem all that excited by my news. Papá and I were not on good terms, but we'd reached a standoff, ignoring each other rather than clashing. He wasn't very supportive of my interest in band—sometimes he'd "forget" I had a concert and be off with the car, so I'd be late. That would embarrass me and make Mami mad, but Papá kept doing it.

My parents were pleased by my award, but they didn't really understand why the drums were such a big deal or why the award mattered so much to me. As far as Mami was concerned, music was melody and song. But I loved being the timekeeper, breaking musical moments into beats for everyone in the band to follow.

Mario tried to tell them how important the award was. "It's a big deal," he told them. "You should be proud." My parents' friends even came over and tried to explain, but I didn't think Mami and Papá ever really understood what winning that competition meant to me. I had to be excited for myself. And I was.

Winning the award meant that when I started high school, in tenth grade, I was automatically made the first chair percussion player. At that time, very few girls were encouraged to play percussion. And when they did, they were given melodics, such as xylophone or glockenspiel, to play, not a drum set or timpani. But I didn't care. I'd earned my place in the band, and I loved it. And I loved playing the drums.

That year, I played snare drum in the marching band and timpani in the concert band. Then, in the spring, the school received a set of timbales for the marching band. These were three drums that the player wore with a harness that went around the player's back. They were loud!

Since I was already the first chair, I assumed I'd be playing the timbales in the marching band that fall. But when I mentioned this to the band director, Mr. Ramsey, he said they were too heavy for me. They were thirty or thirty-five pounds, a third of my weight. I was a girl, and he couldn't take the chance that I could hurt myself while playing them.

That was not an answer I could accept. I was a girl, and I was looking after our car. I was a girl, and I was getting good grades in math and science and planning to go to college. I was going to play the timbales in the fall, and I knew I had to convince Mr. Ramsey that I could do it.

But instead of arguing, I made a plan. A few days later, school let out for the summer. The next day, I rode my bike to the high school. Even though it was June and the sun beat down on me, I was wearing a heavy coat, with weights in the pockets. I'd brought more weights in my bike basket, pieces of metal and heavy stones that I'd found around our house and yard. I parked my bike and went to the back, onto the football field. Then I marched around the track, carrying those weights in my arms, determined to build up the muscles in my legs, arms, and back.

At the end of an hour, I was hot, sweaty, and tired. But the next day, I did it again, and the day after that, too. For an hour, every single day that summer, I marched around the track. Mario told me I was weird for training this way, but by the end of August, I was ready.

On the first day of school, I found the music director in the band room and told him I wanted to play the timbales in the marching band. Mr. Ramsey started to protest, and I told him that I'd show him, then and there, that I could do it.

The harness for the timbales buckled on with a wide leather hip strap and shoulder straps. The drums were easy to lift into the harness. I could tell I'd gotten strong over the summer.

When you were marching with the timbales during the halftime show at a football game, you had to stop on each line marker and then rock back. To do that, you had to have strong muscles, especially in your legs.

We went outside to the football field, where the players were warming up. I strapped on the timbales. I began to march up and down the sideline, turning, twisting, rocking back, while playing the timbales. My summer work had paid off, and I barely felt the weight of the drums.

After a few minutes, Mr. Ramsey shook his head. "Okay, you can play the timbales," he said, "but people will be mad at me for letting a girl carry these heavy drums." He told me he would start me in the timbales position in the marching band. If I couldn't handle it, he warned me, he would replace me — and fast. And he made one of the tallest and largest boys in the band, who played the smallest instrument, the piccolo, march beside me in case I fell down.

Of course I never fell down or needed any help with the timbales. I made sure of that — that is, after I figured out how to handle them. They really were big and bulky, and if I swung around too quickly, I could hit someone.

But once I understood how to move with the drums strapped in place, they gave me tremendous power. With the timbales, you could control the band, even control the stadium by starting cheers. You could do a drumroll and get everybody's attention. I loved playing the timbales! I couldn't always control what was happening at home, but with the music, I was in charge.

Even before I started high school, I felt pulled between different worlds: home and school, Spanish and English, traditional and modern. At home, we spoke Spanish and lived in a culture where girls like me respected their parents, learned to keep house, and planned to marry soon after graduating from high school. When I saw my old friends from Bradley Elementary School, who still lived in our old neighborhood, they talked about boys they had crushes on, about older girls who had gotten married. They wore pretty dresses and talked a lot about hairstyles and makeup. They looked forward to their quinceañeras, and they almost never talked about school.

I cared about those friends—after all, I'd known them all my life. Sometimes I saw them in the teen group that Mami ran at our church. But by the time I was in middle school, I felt like a weird, nerdy girl when I was with them. Because we'd left Griggs Street for a home in a different neighborhood so many years earlier, I was used to moving in a world where most of the people I saw every day were Anglo, not Mexican.

Starting when I was in second grade and enrolled at Alameda Elementary School, many of the girls I knew were from homes that weren't quite as traditional as mine. Still, most of them didn't plan to go to college. Even many of my Girl Scout friends didn't think about going to college. It wasn't until junior high that I met other girls like me, girls who liked math and thought it would be fun to work at a job and earn a living. They reminded me of the girls I sometimes saw on television, who had adventures. I liked having friends who thought the way I did, and their confidence reinforced my own.

By the time I was in high school, I was making steady progress toward my goal of college. When I could, I worked at odd jobs and saved my pay. I had good grades and money in the bank, and I'd never forgotten my fourth-grade teacher's words when I'd told her I wanted to go to Stanford University. "You're a smart girl. If you want to go there, you can." These days, I looked forward to my schoolwork and enjoyed mastering new concepts and ideas and showing what I could do.

I still spent time with my family, but in junior high and high school, I had a lot of homework. Some weekends, there'd be a fiesta in the park. My whole family would go, and I was expected to go with them, even though I had homework. The fiesta would last for hours, but after a while, Mami would let me sit in the car and read. Sometimes Papá would complain and say I should be with the family, but Mami always supported me.

When I was in eleventh grade, Mario left home. He'd been accepted to the West Point military academy, far away in New York. And while he was adjusting to life as a cadet, I was still having a running battle with Papá.

Over the years, Papá had left most of the day-to-day decisions about raising us to Mami. He cared that we got good grades in school, but he paid much more attention to Mario and Armando than he did to Laura and me. With his high standards for education, he encouraged me to think about college, but at the same time, he seemed to expect that I would get married right after graduating high school, like most of the women around us. And as if that was not confusing enough, he also expected that when I turned fifteen, I would have a quinceañera.

The other girls I knew from Mexican families looked forward for years to their quinceañeras. This party celebrated a girl's passage into womanhood. She wore a white dress—almost like a wedding dress—jewelry, makeup, and a glamorous hairstyle. She was presented on the arm of an eligible young man, and she was expected to dance and have a wonderful time.

Papá knew I was more interested in getting good grades and planning for college than in finding a husband. But he still thought I should have a quinceañera. And I thought I should not. By now, I identified much more strongly with the world of school, college, and achievement, even though I knew that some married women, like my Tía Alma, a teacher, had been to college and had good jobs.

In my mind, I was a nerdy girl who shot off rockets in the desert, and I dreamed of walking on lush green lawns between the red-roofed, tan, and arched buildings of Stanford University. To me, a quinceañera represented a traditional world that had no place for me. So my father and I would argue, and I would retreat to my bedroom and do math problems to calm myself down. Then I would try to figure out a way around Papá's objections.

Meanwhile, when my older brother returned from his first semester in college, he brought us all extravagant Christmas presents.

He gave my father moleskin pants from L.L.Bean. Papá wore them so much, my mother called them his second skin. Mario gave Mami a beautiful alpaca wool cloak. In the winter, she loved to wrap herself in it.

And Mario gave me real leather athletic shoes from Puma. When I opened the gift, I was speechless. They were the kind of shoes professional athletes wore. I had never told my brother how much sports meant to me, but it was as if he somehow knew.

Mario and I had been so competitive as children, and over the years, I had learned to tune out his teasing. He never let me forget the time I added too much salt to the peanut butter cookies when I was working on my Cooking badge. And we'd bickered many times about other things. Not only that, but in our household and culture, where boys were favored, things came easily to Mario, while I had to find my own way to get what I wanted. My family loved me, but they didn't understand me, and I often felt like an outsider in my own home.

On that Christmas morning, holding that remarkable gift, I understood that I no longer had to compete with Mario. My brother was on my side. Mario had been exposed to so many new things at West Point, and he wanted to share them with us. But that wasn't all. The very first check he ever wrote was to me, for seventy-five dollars. He wanted a better life for me.

And in the end, with Mami's help, I figured out what to do about the quinceañera. Mami might have preferred that I be a more traditional daughter, but she supported me when I said I would not have the party. Instead, to placate Papá, she bought me a special purple dress. She made me put on makeup and had my hair styled, and we arranged to have a professional photograph taken. And I gave that photograph to my father. He would have to be proud of it, because that was all I would do.

A photograph for Papá

With the timbales in marching band

CHAPTER 17

Against Expectations

Even if Papá expected me to get married, he and Mami still wanted my brother and me to go to college, but they didn't have the money to send us. I was just finishing tenth grade when Mario graduated from high school. With his acceptance to West Point, the United States Army would be paying for his education. I wasn't interested in joining the army, and West Point, like the other military academies, didn't accept women at the time. I knew I would have to find a way to pay for college myself.

During all the years since I'd first started my savings account with the eight dollars in my cat bank, my balance had grown significantly. I didn't have the full cost of a college education, but I had a couple of thousand dollars, a fortune in those days. I was on my way.

It had been a long time since I'd had to rely on finding pennies, nickels, and dimes behind sofa cushions or in the coin-return slots of pay phones. These days, I was earning the money I deposited into my bank account. During the summer between tenth and eleventh grades, my friend Cynthia and I worked as paid baseball umpires. I also took on another job stocking inventory in a store.

But that wasn't all. Whenever Cynthia and I had a free moment, we rode our bikes around Las Cruces, collecting aluminum cans. We knew that the grocery store would pay us a dime for every three cans we turned in. We soon learned which parks to hit, especially after the weekends, when the ground was littered with soda and beer cans.

I deposited everything I earned into the bank. Cynthia and I were both determined to go to college, and we often compared notes about our growing savings accounts.

Between earning money, schoolwork, band, and my friends, I was busy. In addition, while I had not been involved with a Girl Scout troop myself for a few years, I still assisted Mami with Laura's troop. I loved helping Laura and her friends earn a few of the badges that I had earned in Juniors. It took them longer than the girls in my troop to master all the steps, but they learned they could do it, just as I had. Laura was proudest of her Cooking badge and the spaghetti she made for our family.

And when Laura sewed a badge onto her sash, she was like any other Girl Scout. She fit right in!

I tried to find time for Armando too. He was a high-spirited, playful little boy who liked to run around, just as I had when I was his age. I would shoot hoops with him in our driveway, on the court I'd built myself. Over the years, I'd discovered baseball, and I loved to throw a ball against a cinder-block wall, fielding it on the rebound. Armando and I would play catch, challenging each other to harder or higher throws in our backyard.

Armando had another talent that I thought was ingenious. When he was very young, he figured out that his favorite toys, Tonka trucks, would be on sale after Christmas at prices our family could afford. He would tell Mami he didn't want any presents on Christmas Day. Instead, he asked if they could go shopping the next day so he could get one of the expensive trucks. Even though we teased him for not having many gifts under the tree, Armando always held firm, and on the twenty-sixth of December, he and my mother would head out to the toy store. I marveled at his foresight and restraint.

After my father won his lawsuit and my parents had some extra money, they gave Armando a plastic Big Wheel for Christmas one year in addition to his beloved Tonka truck. The surprise that year was that Laura fell in love with Armando's Big Wheel. We loved watching her joy as she wheeled it around the house and driveway. We laughed so hard, even my stoic father had tears streaming down his face as Laura steered the Big Wheel, reveling in the attention.

By the time I was a senior in high school, I had been in band for many years. I really enjoyed playing the timbales in marching band, and each year I had tried out for All-State Band and been accepted.

Then, that fall, I tried out for All-State Band one last time. To my surprise, when they announced the students who'd been selected, my name wasn't on the list. I hadn't made the cut. I was devastated. I had been so certain I was going to make the list, just as I had every other year. I was heartbroken.

I spent the weekend sitting in front of the fireplace, reading a big book of college majors that I had checked out from the library, trying not to think of my friends in All-State Band missing school in the coming week to attend rehearsals. On Friday, knowing those friends would be in Albuquerque, preparing for the big concert, I couldn't force myself to go to school.

I sat at home with the college book, thinking hard, trying to distract myself from picturing my friends having fun at All-State. I remembered how much I had enjoyed earning my Science badge in Girl Scouts. I had enjoyed designing and building my basketball backboard too. I liked math, and I was good at it. I knew I wanted to study something in college that used math or science. I was interested in engineering, also.

I read about several different kinds of engineering majors: civil, mechanical, and electrical. Then I saw a mention of industrial engineering. It was described as a mix of people and processes, systems and how people work with them. It required a special facility in math, which I thought I had.

I liked working with people, and I knew a lot about how to do so from watching Mami with Laura's and my Girl Scout troops. I was organized and knew how to plan, because of the Girl Scouts.

I could be an industrial engineer!

I looked up colleges and universities that had programs in industrial engineering. Many universities had engineering schools, but few of them offered industrial engineering. But to my surprise, I found that New Mexico State University, right in Las Cruces, had a program. I hadn't put aside my dreams of Stanford, but I could at least learn more about engineering much closer to home.

My book listed the name of the dean and a phone number. I quickly called and made an appointment for that very day. I'd gotten my driver's license a few months earlier, so I borrowed the family car and drove over to the university. Papá was at work, and Mami didn't ask any questions about where I was going.

The dean was surprised that I knew about industrial engineering. One of his first questions was about my grades. Fortunately, I could tell him that I had straight As and was in the top ten in my class.

"Okay, but you are a girl. Are you sure you want to be an engineer?" he asked. I was surprised by his question. Why wouldn't I want to be an engineer, just because I was a girl? I told him what I had learned and why I was interested in industrial engineering.

Once the dean understood that I'd done some real research into his field, he told me a bit more about industrial engineering. *Industrial engineering makes people's lives better,* he said. That sounded all right to me. I left his office that day feeling enthusiastic about my plan for a college major.

But just because I had settled on a field of study didn't mean I was ready for college. First, I had to figure out how to pay for it. By now I realized that college cost far more than I'd be able to save by the time I graduated high school. The dean had told me that New Mexico State had a four-year scholarship for engineers, and I applied, filling out paperwork that included many questions about my math and science education.

After I sent in the application, I received a call from my high school principal's office. Two engineers were being sent to my school to interview me because I was a girl. They wanted to test me to see if it was really me who had filled out the paperwork for the scholarship. They had expected only boys to apply, and they wanted to make sure I was serious about being an engineer—the way they expected a boy would be. They were afraid that I might take this prestigious scholarship and then get married and leave the field.

Of course both of the engineers were men, and one of them was not at all happy to be interviewing a girl. "How do you know you can do engineering?" he asked me. "Give me one example."

"I know how to maintain cars," I said, thankful that the dean had taken the trouble to tell me about the engineering program and what engineers actually did. "I know how to change our car's oil."

"Go step by step," the man said, challenging me. "Explain it to me."

So I did.

When I finished, he said, "No, you've just seen your dad and your brother do it."

I laughed at that! I told them that my father had never changed the oil in our cars—he didn't even know how to do it! Then I told those engineers how much I enjoyed math and how earning Girl Scout badges had taught me how to be organized and prepare for problems. I even talked about how much trouble I'd had with the Science and Cooking badges and how I'd solved one problem after another.

In the end, I must have convinced them. As they left that day, one of them said to me, "You represent change." He told me he thought I might make a good engineer, though he also cautioned me that "change for the sake of change is not progress." I wasn't sure what he meant, because I thought that letting girls become engineers was definitely progress! But I never forgot what he said, because even though he'd been skeptical, he was willing to give me a chance.

I still had my dream of Stanford University, but Stanford was awfully far away, and I knew the money I'd saved wouldn't be nearly enough. And even though I was near the top of my class, proud of my Mexican heritage, there were no other girls among our family's friends or at our church who also wanted to be an engineer. At school and at home, everyone thought it would be nice if I attended college, but I wasn't given much practical help. I had to face the truth: I couldn't afford Stanford.

It was time to set my sights on colleges that I could afford to attend. I would need to get as much financial aid as I could. And to pay for what my scholarships wouldn't cover, I continued to build my nest egg.

And then, the winter of my senior year, the phone rang in the middle of the night. My mother answered it, and a minute later she screamed and burst into tears. When she could talk, she told us the terrible news: her mother, Abuelita Leonor, had passed away.

My grandmother had been visiting one of my aunts in Los Angeles. She had had a cold that had turned into pneumonia. She called my aunt to her side and said that she felt she was not going to make it, and she needed to call their pastor at church. Then she closed her eyes. My aunt called the paramedics and the pastor, but it was too late. By the time the ambulance got there, Abuelita Leonor was gone.

My mother was devastated by her mother's death. I didn't know this grandmother as well as my Abuelita Juanita, my father's mother, who lived in Las Cruces. Still, I was surprised at how sad I felt. My grandmother had always been nice to me, making my favorite cookies whenever we visited her in Mexico. It was hard to believe that I'd never see her again.

Because Abuelita Leonor had been overweight, we were told that it would cost extra money to bring her body back home. She would need a special casket, and that would be very expensive.

It was without question that our family would do whatever it took for her to be buried properly. At the time, my parents still didn't have much in the way of savings. They didn't even have a credit card, and it wasn't easy to get a loan from the bank. We needed cash.

In my family, it was expected that if someone had a problem, everyone would contribute resources to find a solution. I had a bank account, and I wanted my grandmother to have what she needed. There was only one thing I could do.

My parents were going to drive to Los Angeles that day to arrange for the funeral, but first, my father drove me to the bank so that we could be there when it opened. Then I emptied my savings account and gave all the money I'd saved to my family.

I was disappointed, but I wasn't angry. My family came first. That was the way it had always been and always would be.

Okay, I thought. *I'm not giving up.*

My parents took off to make the long drive to Los Angeles. Left at home with neighbors to help watch over Laura and Armando, I decided that weekend that I would have to work even harder to keep my grades up in hopes of a scholarship.

I did the research, and I applied for all kinds of financial aid. I ended up receiving the engineering scholarship for which I'd interviewed first, which covered four years at New Mexico State University and internships every summer at Sandia National Laboratories, an important defense laboratory in Albuquerque. I was pleased—though I still wished I had figured out a way to attend Stanford. But I was proud that those engineers who'd interviewed me had decided that I was right for their program. I had earned their respect, and they had given me my chance to go to college.

But that wasn't all. Because I had a good academic record, in the end I was awarded quite a few scholarships, more than I needed.

I didn't keep them, though. My mother made me give them all back.

"You can't be greedy. You have enough," she said.

"These are opportunities for other kids." I could have used the money, but once we knew I had a full scholarship, Mami wouldn't let me keep the rest.

So I headed off to college with just enough scholarship money — and not a cent more.

I never realized how much I liked having a role in the Christmas food preparation until my first semester of college. After final exams, I was tired, but on that first morning home, Mami woke me up, saying I was needed for the tamales. I could smell the red chile sauce, and a warm feeling of belonging washed over me. Later, I would go with my mom to the senior home where Hermana Díaz lived now to deliver freshly made tamales and other homemade holiday goodies.

And when that first college vacation was over, I had something else to look forward to. Title IX, the law that mandated schools and colleges must create equal educational opportunities for girls, including sports teams, had passed when I was in high school. While my high school eventually had a girls' basketball team, it hadn't happened during my time there. I had continued to play on my own and to practice, though, because I still loved the game.

Soon after I started college, I saw a notice that a women's basketball team was holding tryouts. It felt like a dream come true. At the appointed hour, I went to the gym, wearing my athletic clothes and best tennis shoes. I saw other girls dressed in basketball gear with shorts and tank tops emblazoned with team names, and I realized that, unlike me, they must have played on formal teams in high school. For just a minute, I wondered how I could ever compete with them—but I was determined to try.

A blond woman with a whistle around her neck was passing out clipboards and forms. She was Coach Fey, the head coach. I looked at the form that she'd handed me and easily filled in my name, address, and college major. Then came the hard part.

What were my average statistics? I saw spaces for points scored, rebounds, steals, and minutes per game. There was a space for awards and recognition. I had nothing to fill in. I handed my mostly blank form back to Coach Fey, and she shook her head.

Was she really going to keep me from trying out, just

because I'd never had the chance to play on a team in high school?

"Coach Fey, I never miss a lay-up," I said with confidence.

She gave me a long look, taking in the fact that besides my lack of competitive experience, I was much shorter than the other girls. Then she tilted her head in the direction of the court. "Okay, you can try out," she said. I grinned and sprinted across the gym.

In the end, compared to some of the girls with more experience, I wasn't a star player, but I did manage to make the varsity team. I was mostly a benchwarmer, sitting at the edge of the court and watching the better players, but I didn't care. Even though the practices were hard and challenging, I loved them. I loved being on a team at last, and I even got to go on road trips.

As for the games themselves, usually the only time I touched a ball was in the warm-ups. One night, though, the coach looked down the bench and motioned for me to check in. I was so excited. Soon, while on defense, I was able to steal the ball and drive the length of the court for a lay-up.

Everyone on the team was so happy that the benchwarmer had scored! In the next timeout huddle, Coach Fey congratulated me.

"Coach, I told you, I never miss a lay-up," I replied.

That game felt like the culmination of all those Sundays in our driveway, shooting until I had made that hundredth lay-up before I went inside to watch *The Wonderful World of Disney*. In those days, I didn't know that I'd ever find a way to play on a team, but I'd worked hard anyway because I loved basketball so much.

By the end of my second semester of college, I discovered that while I loved playing basketball, I loved my engineering classes more. Even though it was just for one season, I was thankful that I had been able to live out my passion for playing basketball. After that season, I knew my path lay in the classroom and not on the court.

*High school graduation with
my friend Cynthia Schramm*

Me working on the Tonopah Test Range, Nevada, 1975

CHAPTER 18

Being a Rocket Scientist and Realizing My Dream of Stanford

The longest ride I ever took alone with Papá was before my freshman year in college, when he drove me to a summer internship at Sandia National Laboratories in Albuquerque, New Mexico.

Papá and I had clashed many times over the years. Though he was proud of my achievements, I just didn't fit his idea of a traditional daughter, and I never would. He made no secret of favoring Mario and Armando, and he was gentle and affectionate with Laura. But he didn't know what to do with me.

He seemed happier in his work toward the end of my high school days. After he won his lawsuit, he'd been promoted, and he became known for his expertise in handling biohazard material. At home, we weren't arguing furiously anymore.

Still, my father and I didn't often spend time alone together. I was a little nervous before the drive. What would we have to say to each other? It didn't occur to me then that he might be nervous too.

The four-hour drive from Las Cruces to Albuquerque was probably the best time I ever had with my father. He talked the entire way, but he gave me great advice about working in a laboratory, because he had worked in one too.

We both knew I was likely to be the only woman in the lab. There just weren't many women working in the sciences or engineering in those days. I was determined to succeed, but Papá and I knew I would meet people who wouldn't approve of what I was doing, and he wanted me to know what could happen.

He wanted to prepare me for hazing, for being sent off on wild-goose chases or made the victim of silly pranks. He must have known that while all new workers were teased,

I'd be set up for more of this because I was a woman. He gave me lots of advice, in a monologue, because that was how he talked.

He told me never to complain, no matter what the working conditions were like. He warned me not to get upset, even if my coworkers seemed to be taunting me. The men who worked in the lab weren't used to being around girls with math and science interests, he said. Not only would I have to perform my job flawlessly, but I would have to show them I wouldn't be bothered by anything that was said around me. As a woman and as a Mexican American, Papá said, I would be judged by a higher standard.

I welcomed his advice, but I was shocked. Papá had never, ever spoken to me like this before, never taken the trouble with me that he had with Mario. It was almost as if he were seeing me for the first time, not as some girl who wouldn't accept a quinceañera, but as *me*.

In the end, I was glad for my father's advice. In my very first meeting at the laboratory, I was shown into a room full of engineers who were seated around a table. I was not even given a place to sit down. Papá had told me just to find ways to be helpful and make everyone's job easier, so I didn't show that this bothered me.

My first summer internship involved field-testing rockets. They'd never had a woman engineer, so they didn't even have a bathroom for women in the test labs. I had to use the restrooms in the building where the secretaries worked, so I had to plan my breaks accordingly. I brought in a bicycle so that I could make it there quickly. I had to stay organized! Finally they gave me my own portable bathroom, complete with a sign that simply said HERS.

I wasn't surprised, either, when it turned out there were no engineers' coveralls that fit me. These were large, heavy garments designed for men—big men. I used duct tape to adjust the pants and sleeves on my coverall and to make the gloves stay on my hands. The lab had to special order me a pair of Red Wing steel-toe boots like the other engineers wore, because the shoes didn't come in women's sizes.

I was a little surprised to find that these things didn't bother me. They were obstacles to overcome, but they had nothing to do with the work of engineering, which I loved.

After all, I'd flown Estes model rockets for my Girl Scout Science badge. Now I got to work on the real thing. Finding a way to make the coverall fit was just a small problem to be solved so I could get back to being an engineer!

In my second summer, I was put to work designing and drawing. Nowadays engineers do this on computers, but back then, we had to draw our models by hand. During my third summer, I worked in the laboratory, and during my fourth year, I learned about the human factors involved in engineering. My analysis of tracking radioactive shipments in the United States was included in a presentation to Congress.

After I graduated college, my boss wrote a beautiful note to my parents thanking them for doing a good job raising me. The note went on to say that young people like me gave him confidence in the future, because he knew the world would be in good hands. My parents were proud of me, but by now, I knew it was more important that I was proud of myself.

Looking back, I find it a little surprising that I worked as a rocket scientist at all, since in those days it was so rare for women to have opportunities like that. But one reason I succeeded was that I wasn't afraid of math. To do the kind of complex math problems that are required in rocket science, you have to understand algorithms—multistep problems—at a high level. When I was in high school and college, very few students, especially girls, got as far as calculus, the advanced math that's one of the first steps in an engineering education. Calculus problems are complicated, and many students are intimidated by them. But when I figured out how to solve one, I had a wonderful feeling of accomplishment.

In some ways, I had been preparing to be a rocket scientist and engineer ever since the days when I counted to myself in English and Spanish as I walked to my lessons with Hermana Díaz. I liked math and numbers even before I learned to read, even before I spoke many words in English.

In middle school, when I took algebra instead of home economics, I was preparing for my career, though I didn't realize it at the time. Back then, I really didn't want to grow up to be a housewife. And fortunately for me, I also liked solving math problems!

. . .

After college, armed with my degree in industrial engineering, I heard about an opening for a job as an engineer at the Jet Propulsion Laboratory (JPL) in Pasadena, California. Because of my summer internship experience at the Sandia labs, I was hired.

The first program I worked on was called the Solar Polar Solar Probe (try saying that five times fast!), or SPSP for short. I was hired to help figure out the payload and testing equipment that would be carried on a satellite going to the sun. How would the equipment work in the intense heat generated close to the sun? How would it react to the radiation? How would its weight affect the amount of fuel that we would need to carry on the rocket? To answer these questions, I had to create complex algorithms—like very difficult word problems. And then I had to solve them.

It takes a long time—a very long time—to launch a new space expedition. The solar probe that I was working on wouldn't be ready for launch for more than thirty years—sometime in 2018.

Meanwhile, after a time, I was assigned to another project at JPL, the Voyager 2 flyby of Jupiter. This was a long-range program, that continues to this day, sending automated spacecraft to the outer planets and beyond to record data and send it back to Earth. The Voyager spacecraft was transmitting amazing images and data, and JPL needed engineers to analyze them.

At the time, we didn't have personal computers at our desks with the software to perform all the necessary analyses. Those computers and that software hadn't been invented yet. Instead, young engineers were assigned to identify the variables in the data coming back from Jupiter. Then we could write the programs that would allow the large mainframe computers available back then to process the new data from Voyager. This was quite a task, but I continued to love what I did. It was an exciting project because we could go into the cafeteria to see the images of the distant planet and moons that were being transmitted from the spacecraft.

Through my years in college and working as a rocket scientist, I hadn't forgotten my dream of Stanford. While I was still at New Mexico State University, I was honored to be asked to join the engineering honor society, Tau Beta

Pi. I even was elected president. I had wanted to assume a leadership position because I felt so strongly about being an engineer and wanted to support other students who were choosing this course of study. Not all of the other students were enthusiastic about my candidacy. But I worked hard, and I was voted into the position, the first woman to be president of my chapter. I thought at the time, and I still think, that my experience earning Girl Scout badges, selling cookies, and working as a team with other girls in my troop gave me the confidence to be a leader.

After college graduation, although I was excited about the position at the Jet Propulsion Laboratory, I was also interested in graduate school. I took the Graduate Record Examinations — tests required for admission into graduate programs — and then I applied to the graduate engineering program at Stanford University. Soon I received a letter of congratulations in the mail: I was admitted! Once again, all I had to do was figure out how to pay for it.

Then something happened that still seems like a miracle to me. I had been searching for scholarships to cover the cost of graduate school, but I wasn't having any luck. The phone rang one afternoon, and I heard a man's voice asking if I was Sylvia Acevedo. Then he said, "My name is Dr. Howard Adams from the National GEM Consortium. We want to offer you a fellowship to cover the cost of your graduate study at Stanford."

He explained that the GEM Consortium—the National Consortium for Graduate Degrees for Minorities in Engineering and Science—funded the education of underrepresented groups for graduate study in the STEM fields of science, technology, engineering, and mathematics. I realized that they must have gotten my name from the graduate school at Stanford. As a young Latina studying engineering, I was just the candidate that GEM was looking for. What I hadn't realized was that financial aid for graduate school was called a fellowship, not a scholarship. No wonder I hadn't had any luck finding funds!

That day, on the phone, Howard Adams explained his organization to me: "We don't know you personally. But we know what promise you represent." He meant that with people like me—women and those from underrepresented groups—entering the STEM fields, not only would the companies we worked for benefit, but society as a whole would be stronger. I believed him, and that helped me believe in myself.

GEM's fellowship represented a promise to myself as well. It meant my childhood dream of attending Stanford would be coming true.

At Stanford, studying industrial and systems engineering using computer science, I found myself at the dawn of an era. Much was quickly changing since the days when computers were mainframes that took up entire large rooms. Back then, to run a program, you had to punch holes in cards—stacks of them—that were then fed into the computer. After the program ran, results were printed out on sheets of green-and-white-lined paper.

Most people, especially ordinary citizens, didn't have access to computers in those days. I was a graduate engineering student at the very beginning of a time when computers were redesigned to be smaller and more portable and personal. It would be many years before the Internet was in common use. But Stanford is in what is now known as Silicon Valley. It was ground zero, exactly where the computer revolution was beginning to transform our society.

Stanford University was at once like my dreams and nothing like them. The university looked a great deal like the picture I'd seen many years earlier in my fourth-grade classroom. But I was one of the few women, and one of a very few Latinos, in the graduate school of engineering. The other graduate students were from the best schools in the world. Many of my classmates had been personally selected by the highest levels of their government to represent their country at Stanford. For once, I felt intimidated.

There was only one answer: I would have to work harder than I ever had before. And I did.

In many ways, I never really left home until I went to Stanford. After my first year at New Mexico State University, I moved home from the dormitories and commuted to college. I felt I still had a responsibility to help bring up my younger brother and sister, like any daughter in a traditional Mexican family. But now I would be in California for at least a year, and I already knew that after I earned my graduate degree, I would not be moving back home. To find work in the fields that interested me, I would almost certainly have to move away from Las Cruces — and from my family. I would miss them, but I wanted to see what I could do.

I also knew that I wouldn't be saying goodbye to my family just because I wouldn't be living at home. After all, my mother had also left her family, but she had never forgotten them. They were all still very much a part of our lives. I would always feel the pull of my family in New Mexico, and I would always stay close to them.

After I was admitted to Stanford, Papá would brag about me to anyone who would listen. If someone happened to remark about his coffee cup with the university's logo on its side, he would say, "Oh, have I told you about my daughter who's studying at Stanford?"

He would never admit in my presence how proud he was of me. Papá might have wished he had a daughter who celebrated a real quinceañera, who grew up to be a mother and wife and never dreamed of working outside the home. That wasn't me — but in the end, he was proud of the daughter he had.

Mami was proud of me too, but in a different way. Because she didn't grow up in the United States, and because she never received a traditional education, the prestige of a particular college mattered less to her than to Papá. She didn't really care if I went to New Mexico State or to Stanford University, as long as I got an education. Her question for me, no matter what I achieved, was "Are you happy?" And, as I finally realized, Mami asked the only question that really mattered.

At my graduation from Stanford

EPILOGUE

To my readers . . .

Last night, I looked outside and saw a beautiful full moon hanging low over the tall buildings of New York City. It was the same moon that shone above our neighborhood of unpaved dirt streets in Las Cruces, over my first Girl Scout camping trip, above the desert at Sandia National Laboratories, and over the well-kept lawns of Stanford University.

Like the moon, you have come with me on my journey as I have relived my early years. I have enjoyed thinking about my childhood and all the ways that I have been shaped by my family and my culture—sometimes even by defying that culture.

When I was a very little girl, if I thought much about my future, it was to imagine that I would do interesting things and have adventures. From the makeshift classroom with Hermana Díaz at La Primera Iglesia Bautista to my early days in Head Start to the many wonderful teachers I met in school, I learned to love learning, something I enjoy to this day.

Through the Girl Scouts and the family and friends who helped me along the way, I learned to create opportunities for myself. My family didn't have much money, but I found that if I worked hard and pursued an education, new possibilities would continue to unfold. Through my parents, brothers, and sister, I learned the importance of family and caring for others.

I also drew strength from my heroes, women I had read about as a child, such as Clara Barton, Eleanor Roosevelt, Florence Nightingale, Amelia Earhart, and Helen Keller. I learned from them that we all—rich and poor—struggle against adversity. I also learned that everyone needs help sometimes. I got a lot of help along the way, and I came to understand how to take responsibility for myself. We are each responsible for our own fate, and with help from others, we can achieve success if we plan well and work hard.

There is one other source of inspiration that I could not do without, and that is you! I love speaking to groups of young people. I'm continually impressed with your energy, with your passion to improve the world, and by your stories.

In the mid-2000s, someone who was studying in the Stanford archives asked to interview me. I was one of the first—and few—men or women of Latino heritage to have gotten a graduate degree in engineering from Stanford. I was asked how it was that, as a Latina, I was prepared to do the advanced math and science required at the graduate level at Stanford. And how had I even known about Stanford, since they didn't recruit in Las Cruces at that time?

As I answered the interviewer's questions, I was reminded once more of how much of my experience stemmed from Girl Scouts. Learning how much cooking was like science as I earned my badges gave me the experience and the confidence to pursue my interests, even if they were not shared by most other girls. Until the Stanford interview, I had never realized that my love of reading, which began during my time in Head Start, and the curiosity, love of science, and confidence that I gained in Girl Scouts had made such a difference in my life. Those childhood experiences changed everything for me.

I was so grateful for that interview and for what it taught me that I became a passionate advocate for early childhood education and the Girl Scouts. Eventually, my work in education led me to serve as a commissioner on the White House Initiative on Educational Excellence for Hispanics, where I chaired the Early Learning subcommittee. Then I met former Texas governor Ann Richards, who learned of my interest in Girl Scouts and nominated me for the national board of the Girl Scouts of the USA. My parents and sister had passed away by then, but my brothers, Mario and Armando, and I were ecstatic, knowing the positive impact Girl Scouts had had on our family. The Girl Scouts had given me so much, and now I could give something back to them.

I served on the national board for eight years before being asked to serve as chief executive officer of the Girl Scouts of the United States of America. It is a dream come true, from the deserts of New Mexico to the skyscrapers of New York City.

I hope that my life story will prove to you that dreams *do* come true and that it will inspire you to create your own opportunities and adventures. Have the courage to work to make the world a better place—and I will cheer you on as you do! Thank you.

Love,
Sylvia

Me and President Obama

(Official White House photo by Chuck Kennedy)

A NOTE ABOUT GIRL SCOUTS YESTERDAY AND TODAY

As those of you who are Girl Scouts read my story, you may have discovered that some aspects of my experience with Girl Scouts, fifty-ish years ago, were different from yours. When I joined the Brownies, most girls weren't allowed to wear pants to school, so my Brownie and Junior uniforms included a dress or skirt. There were no Daisies—Brownies was the youngest level of Girl Scouts. And girls couldn't earn badges until they were Juniors. Even the cookies we sell now are different, as tastes have altered over the years.

Other details of Girl Scout life have changed too. At the time that I was a Scout, there were no science badges available for Juniors, so when my troop leader saw my interest in science, she had to suggest I try a Cadette badge. Today, Girl Scouts have made the STEM subjects—science, technology, engineering, and math—a priority, with badges at all Scouting levels.

In my day, the Brownie promise was different from the promise that older Girl Scouts made. Today, Scouts at every level make the same promise. The wording of the Girl Scout Promise and Law has changed as well, but all Scouts, through our entire history, have pledged their service to laws that include honesty, helpfulness, respect for others, and sisterhood with every other Girl Scout.

The Girl Scouts have come a long way since 1912, when Juliette Gordon Low gathered together the first troop of eighteen girls, founding an organization that would prepare young women to meet the world with courage, confidence, and character. My story is just one among those of many millions of girls who have found community, adventure, and purpose in the Girl Scouts.

When adults ask me how their daughters can have the amazing opportunities that I have enjoyed in my life, I encourage them to enroll their daughters in the Girl Scouts.

A girl can join at any age from five to eighteen, and even a few years can make a difference. Girls, their families, and their communities all benefit from involvement in Girl Scouts.

www.girlscouts.org

ACKNOWLEDGMENTS

I remember clearly the day that this book idea was birthed. It was in Austin, Texas, at the Central Texas Girl Scout's Women of Distinction event, when I was asked to provide the keynote address. I decided to speak from the heart about what Girl Scouts meant to me and my family. Girl Scouts was a ray of light when my family's life had been darkened by tragedy. That day, I spoke about my troop leaders, who saw my interest in science, who helped me set goals through selling cookies, who taught me to create opportunity. I spoke about how Girl Scouts changed my life, and the lives of my sister and mother, too. The enthusiastic reaction to that speech gave me the courage to tell my story.

I was privileged to be supported by gracious and generous mentors who saw the promise of my story to inspire a rising generation of young people: Dr. Nora Comstock, community leader, and Adriana Dominguez, my literary agent, have been my indispensible guitjes and connectors on this journey.

My colleagues and friends, Carissa Ara, Christin Alvarado, Marissa Limon, and Doyle Valdez, dutifully listened to so many versions of this story, across the country and in Austin, Texas, that they could tell it themselves. Yet they never lost interest or wavered in their desire to help. And my friend Gail Collins, who has included me in two of her books (*When Everything Changed* and *As Texas Goes...*), offered vital encouragement and advice to this first-time author.

No book is a solo journey, and I have been aided and helped by so many, including my talented co-writer, Ruth Katcher, who captured the feelings, especially adolescent emotional angst, and brilliantly transformed what I had written, recasting it into a compelling story.

My brothers, Armando and Mario, and my Tía Angélica patiently answered many historical questions, dusting off the memories of long-ago family events. My parents and younger sister have passed away, and I leaned heavily on my older brother, Mario, himself a published author, who painstakingly provided edits, advice, and corrections. My cousin Cathy Barba's corrective nuances in both English and Spanish sharpened the narrative. I am grateful to my many relatives, in both of my parents' families, here in the United States and in Mexico. I feel their love and support.

Two organizations, Head Start and the Girl Scouts, were gracious in answering many questions about their programs in the 1960's, providing details that escaped my notice as a young girl. Yasmina Vinci, the Executive Director of Head Start, has been a stalwart on this journey, giving me many opportunities to share my story with Head Start families and staff, a source of invaluable feedback and suggestions. Wanting to make sure we got the details right about Girl Scout badges, programs, uniforms, handbooks, and cookies, Diane Russo and Yevgeniya Gribov at Girl Scouts of the USA were dogged in tracking down historical information. I am grateful for my Girl Scouts colleagues who have been so supportive.

At Clarion Books, Susan Buckheit did a thoughtful, careful copyediting job. I am grateful to the Clarion team as a whole, including Dinah Stevenson, Lisa DiSarro, Amanda Acevedo, Alia Almeida, Veronica Wasserman, Tara Shanahan, Andrea Miller, and Kiffin Steurer, for their dedication and passion for making this the best book possible and getting it into the hands of readers. My gratitude goes to Isabel Mendoza, for her expert and nuanced work crafting the Spanish translation of this book. And I'm especially fortunate to have Anne Hoppe as an editor: her enthusiasm is contagious, and her editorial insight was transformative.

The love and faith of my friends and extended and blended family across the country, and especially in my hometowns of Las Cruces, Menlo Park, Austin, New York, and Santa Barbara have been my mainstays and supporters. You, dear family and friends, patiently listened to my stories and continuously offered encouragement.

Dr. Janet Osimo has made everything else possible. Thank you.

Me as a Brownie

Me as CEO of the Girl Scouts of the USA